VALERIA S

ANDY WOOD

TO LIVE, DIE AND SHINE IN PRE-GRUNGE SEATTLE

LEDIZIONI PUBLISHING

Translation from the original: *Andy Wood, l'inventore del grunge. Vivere e morire a Seattle prima dei Pearl Jam*, by Valeria Sgarella. Area 51/Ledizioni Publishing, 2016

Translation and adaptation: Jade Parolini.

Via Boselli, 1 – 20136 Milano – Italy
www.ledizioni.it
info@ledizioni.it

Valeria Sgarella, *Andy Wood. To live, die and shine in pre-grunge Seattle*

First print: march 2022

ISBN: 978-88-5526-643-7

CONTENTS

*In loving memory of Giancarlo,
my father, and of my dear buddy
Gianluca Ferraris, first person to
read this book, in its early drafts.*

"Up to that point, I think life was really good for us, as a group of musicians in a scene making music. Our world was sort of our oyster. We had support, we supported each other. Andy was kind of like this beam of light above it all. And to see him hooked up to machines... that was, I think, the end of the innocence of the scene. It wasn't later when people surmised that Kurt had blown his head off. It was that. It was walking into that room."

Chris Cornell (1964-2017), Pearl Jam Twenty documentary, Cameron Crowe, Sept.2011.

PROLOGUE

Seattle, Washington. Six o'clock of any given evening in 1990. Car radios are tuned to KISW FM 100, the town's rock station. *Get The Led Out* is just minutes away. It's the show feeding several degrees of one's rock appetite, majestically hosted by DJ Mike Jones. When he's in a good mood he throws in at least a half hour of Led Zeppelin.

KISW's claim to fame is "Seattle's Best Rock." Curiously though, the rotation doesn't include much of Seattle's local music, except for *Hands All Over* by Soundgarden.

Get The Led Out's opening theme makes you think of a slow, impressive aerial overview of Seattle.

On Monday, March 19th, 1990, the show's opening sequence isn't the usual one after the ad break. A few hours before air time, Mike Jones has got a phone call from Kelly Curtis, the manager of local bands Alice In Chains and Mother Love Bone. «I'm telling everybody coming up here in the office to listen to your show tonight. I need *you* to break the news.». Kelly's voice trembled with emotion as he went on, "And do you remember the restriction on *Apple*? Well, you now have permission to play all the tracks you want."

Mother Love Bone's debut album *Apple* had been embargoed by Mercury Records. A copy of it had stalled in the music programming office for months, awaiting the label's official release date.

At 6 o'clock sharp, Mike Jones' voice kicked in. It was dry and institutional. Surely it wasn't his usual voice. There was no background music playing.

«Before we start with the show, I've got to share some terrible news with you guys. Andy Wood, the lead singer for Mother Love Bone, has died this morning as a consequence of a heroin overdose. He was just 24.».

From that moment on, to those listening, time flowed in slow-motion.

A whole generation of rock n' roll-fed kids would be stopped in their tracks, stunned.

They would, for the first time, get acquainted with death.

Four years later, the same station would announce Kurt Cobain's death. But the reactions wouldn't be the same.

Those who cried for Andy would not cry again.

The *end of innocence* comes along only once.

PART 1

CHAPTER 1

Hospital rooms

"Is there no God?
So, where are my prayers?".

- Andy Wood, I'm So Cold, ca. 1984

Toni Dahlberg had no idea how women got pregnant. She thought it could happen by praying intensely. So, every night before falling asleep, she would look at the moon and beg God for a little brother or sister.

One day, she heard her parents screaming at each other in the next room. «How the hell do you think I got pregnant? All by myself?», her mom yelled.

Toni felt terribly guilty. Had she been praying too hard? It was her fault, she thought, she had caused this pregnancy.

Toni married Mr. David C. Wood at seventeen. By this point she had figured out you don't get pregnant by praying. Or at least, not *just* that. Toni had known David since they were kids. They had been neighbors in Bremerton, a port city in Washington State, home to the Puget Sound Naval Shipyard. David was a mischievous child; he used to throw stuff onto Toni's porch. It was his way of showing he liked her.

By high school David was one of those cool guys who

smokes and drinks and makes all the girls swoon. Toni would be one of them.

One afternoon, with David and Toni sitting side by side in the car, him at the wheel and her in the passenger seat, a minute and exuberant girl called Patsy declared from the back: «Hey, look at the two of you. You should *definitely* get together». An observation that seemed to come out of nowhere at the time.

Soon after that, David quit school to enlist in the Air Force. He wrote Toni numerous letters, came back home for Christmas, and proposed to her with a big diamond ring. Six months later, they were married.

Patsy had gotten it right.

On her wedding day Toni had cried throughout the entire ceremony. Walking into Our Saviour's Lutheran church in Bremerton, the one where her grandma had forced her to go as a child, she was overwhelmed with delirious joy. Sure, she was young, but eager to start a new life with this boy who had such a strong personality. In those days it was common for women to marry at a young age, often with men they didn't love, just to escape the family home, or out of boredom.

Not Toni, she was deeply in love.

At seventeen, in Bremerton, Pacific Northwest, in the sixties, it didn't really matter to Toni that she didn't know David that well. One thing was for sure: by joining the Air Force, David had committed himself and his newly formed family to a life of never-ending nomadism. Indeed, right after the wedding, the Woods had to move briefly to Kansas, and then relocate overseas to England, at the Burderop Park air base in Wiltshire County, the first in Britain to receive American soldiers during World War II.

Kevin and Brian Wood were born within a year's distance of each other at the USAF hospital at Burderop Park, on September 16th 1961 and October 22nd 1962, both Children Of The Crown. Dave was stationed in an American detachment called Fairford, in Gloucestershire, while Toni and the kids were assigned a place to stay in a picturesque little village called Lechlade-On-Thames. Their apartment was inside an old inn, where the stables used to be.

Each morning the staff of the inn would hang dozens of white sheets out to dry in the garden, and Toni would gaze, mesmerized by their synchronous dance in the wind. And then there were the swans, white processions weaving their way under bridges of stone. And the gardens, overflowing with roses. Toni would take long walks in the village with little Kevin and Brian in their big English double pram, and soak everything in.

Life was good, except they were too poor. Electricity at home ran through a shilling meter, and when there were no shillings, there was only candlelight. If they did have money to power the apartment, they would watch *Bill & Ben The Flowerpot Men* on their fantastic Magnavox TV, sitting snugly in its wooden frame.

Each month, on payday, Toni and the kids would take the bus to the air base to pick up the check. Kevin was all smiles, he loved the double-decker bus.

Respectively ages two and three, Kevin and Brian were the most beautiful, adorable babies. They would sit close to each other on the veranda, wearing identical blue-and-white striped T-shirts, mumbling unintelligible sounds and laughing.

Toni had always wanted kids, many of them, preferably all boys. She had immediately realized she would have to raise them primarily herself; David was gone most of the time, and she often felt the pressure of being a single parent. In spite of this, she loved being a mother and was relatively happy at the time.

After four years in the UK, the Woods moved back to the US. The news was, Toni was pregnant again. Kevin and Brian harbored the idea of having a baby sister, so throughout the pregnancy they would fantasize about her. They had even picked out a name: she would be called Diana Carmen May Wood.

That would have been a whole different story, but things didn't turn out that way.

Andrew Patrick Wood was born on January 8th 1966, in Columbus Air Force Base Hospital, Mississippi. His birth was greeted with joyous celebration by everyone. Well, except for Brian, he was *very* jealous and had no intention of allowing this insolent little squirt to usurp his place as the baby of the family.

Andy's existence would immediately be put to the test, regardless of Brian. Shortly after his birth, on a day like any other, Toni walked up to his room and picked him up from his cradle as always. But something was off: she felt his body stiff, there was no crying for food, no sound or movement coming from him. Upon closer inspection, she saw with terror that his face was drained of blood, his eyes rolled backwards.

Seized with panic, Toni rushed to a neighbor and begged him to drive her to the nearest hospital. At the entrance she was greeted by a number of paramedics who took Andy from her arms, rushing him to intensive care, where she couldn't enter.

Something was horribly wrong with that baby.

Minutes seemed hours as Toni stood in the waiting room. She could see the blue and white scrubs through the window, working on that tiny body, tubes and gauze everywhere.

Poor little Andy.

Life hadn't given him a very warm welcome.

CHAPTER 2

Wartime hero

Kevin, Brian and Andy, Bremerton, WA, ca.1969
[Courtesy of Toni Wood]

«These kids are geniuses».

That's what Toni would regularly claim about Kevin and Brian.

"No, they're criminals", David would promplty reply. "They could get away with murder".

Toni was very indulgent with her children. With David gone most of the time, this meant they basically had no rules. But when David was home, he expected his word to be law.

Whether criminals or geniuses, Kevin and Brian were

nothing alike. Kevin was respectful, polite and never complained, overall a good kid. He tended to steer away from conflict, and rarely lost his temper. When he did, his blind fury exploded on whatever was nearby, so best not to be in his way.

Brian on the other hand was a constant ordeal, always fishing for attention. He had understood from an early age that the best way to get noticed was by misbehaving, and Andy's arrival had only made him more inclined for conflict.

As for Andy, he was a ray of sunshine; ruby red cheeks, ethereal blonde hair, light-blue eyes and a slightly pronounced chin. His expression was one of constant awe, and when, for whatever reason, he was grumpy, he'd look clownish and vaguely comical.

Andy had indeed managed to survive. He had pulled through, but he had been in critical condition. For days, he was closely monitored by doctors and nurses. He had developed a nasty infection in both ears that had spread throughout his body, and as a result, both eardrums had ruptured. The verdict the doctors gave Toni had not been encouraging. "Your son is out of danger, but he could be deaf for the rest of his life."

Deaf. In both ears.

But it wasn't a certain outcome, they'd just have to wait and see.

Throughout this ordeal, David had been overseas of course. When he returned, Andy was still recovering, but the baby's health did not seem to be his main concern.

David had been away during both the labour and the hospital emergency, and when he saw his son for the first time, a nagging doubt started haunting him. How in the hell could this kid have blond hair and blue eyes when both he and Toni had brown hair and eyes?

Toni had never even dared look at another man, and here was David insinuating Andy might be the result of a clandestine affair.

An accusation Toni was not going to forget in the years to come.

Soon it would be time for the Woods to relocate again, this time to Indian Head, Maryland. David had been drafted by EOD, Explosive Ordnance Disposal, and would train for six months at the Naval Ordnance Disposal Unit by the Naval Power Factory.

Toni was still the happiest mother in the world, except for those pesky red ticks, typical of the marshes in Maryland, that kept nesting in her hair. David picked at it every single day, extracting the critters from her thick, curly locks and making her scream in pain.

On those days when he was lazing about on the sofa and didn't want to leave the house, Toni would pile the kids in the car and take them out looking for giant turtles. On one of these expeditions they returned with an unexpected guest: a female Basset Hound puppy. David was still sleeping when they got back, and Toni decided to make the introductions by delicately placing the dog on his stomach, hoping to give him a pleasant surprise.

"What - the - fuck!", was his reaction instead.

As a certified EOD technician, David would be responsible for the safe disposal of explosive devices, either by disarming them, or detonating them where they could do no damage. A high risk and high stakes job.

In 1966, that meant going to Vietnam. He'd gotten orders while the whole family was staying in Columbus. The news disrupted the whole family routine, if ever there was one.

That's what David was destined to. Basically, a helicopter would drop him in the middle of the jungle dressed in civilian clothing, with a fake passport and no identity tags. Officially he knew nothing of the Air Force or any military operations. If anything happened to him, his family wouldn't even be notified.

To his own country, he didn't officially exist.

David himself never spoke about the mission: it was classified information. He wasn't allowed to speak about it. Once away, he would send letters, but they would go through content check at the air base first. In fact, Toni never even knew David was in Vietnam and Laos until he got back. She was told, as general information, that he was in "Southeast Asia".

With David away, Toni took the boys back to Bremerton and lived in the basement of her mom and dad's house. She was relieved to be spending time with her family, as it meant she wasn't alone all the time. Toni also felt useful in mediating the strained relationship between her mother and her kid sister, Stephanie, who was fifteen and pregnant.

Andy at four years old
Courtesy of Toni Wood.

Between the kids and the Basset Hound, which they had called Tami, Toni had her hands full.

Tami got lost everywhere and Toni would regularly receive a phone call from some stranger.

"Hi ma'am. Do you own a Basset Hound?".

"I sure do".

"Well, he's here on the USS Enterprise. If you could come and pick him up, we'd be very grateful", the officer would plead, with a guttural "woof" resounding in the background.

As for the three kids, they were so much fun to be around. Toni felt blessed to have them.

CHAPTER 3

On earth as it is in Texas

"When you are in the US Military, your life and love belong to the US Military. The family never comes first. It's all about FIGMO. Meaning: "Fuck I Got My Orders."

- Toni Wood, interview with the author, 2020

David Wood was a different man when he got back from Vietnam, in the Autumn of 1969. Toni and the kids went to pick him up at the McChord Air Force Base in Tacoma, Washington. They stood there waiting for hours, in a big hangar area, together with other families, hoping to be reunited with their loved ones. As the men stepped down the C-141 Starlifters, Toni could not pick Dave out, among dozens of green uniforms. "Maybe he's not on this plane. Maybe he's on no plane at all", she thought.

And suddenly, there he was.

Toni would never forget his smell, as she hugged him for the first time in one year.

He smelled like war.

What David had seen and experienced in Vietnam, Laos and Cambodia had left a deep wound in his soul and had hardened his heart. Sure, he had saved lives and was even awarded medals, but, in the aftermath, he had become a shadow of the man he used to be. He was intolerant and irascible, everything in his routine now seemed superficial and frivolous. Life as he knew it just didn't suit him anymore.

Toni felt bad for David and what he had to go through, but she also felt herself drifting away from him. She was furious about Vietnam and wished she could march in protest of the war, a shameful page of US history. But she knew that in spite of everything, David wouldn't have approved.

In fact, there were many things David didn't approve of. Such as Toni's musical taste, guilty of being "too black". While David was gone, Toni had total control of the radio and would listen to stations that played blues and soul. But David was all about rock n roll, and now that he was back, it was a whole different tune.

Eventually, David got assigned to the Kerpen USAAF Air Base, in Germany, where American soldiers acted as advisors to the Germans. The Woods were allocated a flat in one of the three blocks of apartments of the American compound. Every relocation took a big effort to complete, but the one to Germany was one of a kind. It required a long, exhausting journey, with a dog and cat in tow, but the Woods made the most of their time on the road. While crossing the country they drove through Pennington County, South Dakota, and stopped by Mount Rushmore, to see the faces of the four former US Presidents carved in stone. A number of tourists were admiring the sculptures from the mountain overlooking the canyon.

That's when Andy, three years old, staged his own show. He ran up to the crowd, arms outstretched, and went like:

"God bless Americaaaa!"

eliciting laughter and cheers from the crowd. Right then and there Toni knew there was a stage in Andy's future. In that exact moment she could envision her son performing in front of an audience, and unlike the tourists, she didn't know whether to laugh or cry.

The very first night in Kerpen was scary. The house was cold, dark and creepy. Kevin and Brian took possession of their respective bedrooms with no hesitation, but Andy ended up crawling into Toni and David's bed in the middle of the night, scaring Toni half to death.

The next morning, determined to carve himself a space in that new setting, Andy put his rubber boots on and walked defiantly towards the front door.

"Hey, where do you think you're going?", Toni enquired.

"I'm going to make new friends", Andy replied confidently.

And off he went, knocking at people's doors in the American compound.

"Hi, I'm Andy, and I'm looking for a friend. You got any kids?".

Toni and the children quickly adapted to the new environment. Toni took German lessons and soon became the official translator for the women of the American compound when they needed to go shopping or run errands. Her German would come in especially handy on the numerous occasions she'd have to go looking for Tami.

«HABEN SIE EINEN GROSSEN HUND MIT LANGEN OHREN GESEHEN?».

Everybody in the Wood family was happily coming to terms with their new life in Germany. Everybody, that is, except David. He didn't seem to fit in with this new setting and was volatile and easily irritated. He and Toni fought often, and it would quickly get physical, fueled by David's excessive alcohol consumption.

There is a long tradition of heavy drinking in the military forces, and David was no exception. In addition, he was growing more and more jealous of Toni, who had become increasingly independent during his prolonged absences.

If he thought he could just leave her for extended periods of time, then reappear and start telling her what to do, well, he had another thing coming.

Sometimes at the parties in the American compound Toni would ask men to dance, just to piss David off. Sometimes those men were black; that would really get him going. He would threaten her. "Don't you dare dance with them niggers or I'll kill you."

As for Andy, his musical crush was Elton John. He simply adored him, fascinated by his flamboyance and spectacular performances. Andy would imitate Elton in the mirror, with his bed as the stage. In his own mind, he was a star.He would tape himself doing fake interviews, as both the interviewer and the interviewee. Sometimes Toni would enter his room way past bedtime and catch him in the middle of a performance, playing air-guitar or simulating a touchdown.

David also used to be into Elton John, but his interest plummeted after a 1976 *Rolling Stone* interview in which he announced he was bisexual. "He's a faggot", David had sentenced.

Not Andy. He wouldn't let something as frivolous as sexual orientation come between him and an artistic infatuation. What did Elton's coming out have to do with the music? "He just got in the wrong line in heaven", Andy would say.

Prior to that *Rolling Stone* interview, David would buy Andy crazy sunglasses like Elton's from every airport he went through, and they had been a lot. Star-shaped, big round ones, in all colors.

But what intrigued Andy the most about Elton, was his piano.

Andy, Brian, Kevin and Tami Kerpen, Germany, ca. 1970]
[Courtesy of Toni Wood]

By 1972, it was time for the Woods to return to the US, namely San Antonio, Texas. David had made up his mind to stop going on missions. Instead, he would train young soldiers to safely dispose of bombs. For that purpose, he first had to attend a school in Tucson, Arizona. It would be a brief stay, during which David would mostly be busy, while Toni was free to drive around Tucson with the kids in her gold Corvette convertible.

By the time they moved to San Antonio, Andy was six years old. The day that sealed the deal on his future was the day he got his first piano.

Andy had insisted he wanted a piano like Elton John's, so David and the kids had purchased one at a local music store - an upright piano in hideous pink - and loaded it onto David's pickup. As they made their way towards home, Kevin and Brian kept a firm grip on the ugly thing to avoid it banging around, while Andy sat and plucked at it with grand, theatrical gestures.

"Watch out for the bend, slow down...
SLOW DOWN!."

David had turned the corner too fast, forgetting the piano was in the back. It tipped over the side of the pickup truck and crashed onto the street. Pieces of piano scattered all over the asphalt, as did Andy's heart.

Once home, the kids moved the piano parts into the garage and David somehow managed to put it back together. After being in charge of detonating unexploded ordnance in Vietnam, fixing a piano was no sweat. And Andy could start taking piano lessons.

David also had his own passions, such as sailing, for example. He was, indeed, a sailor. The problem was that he was so frequently drunk that his boat excursions often turned into extreme and undesired adventures. One time in Bremerton David had been so intoxicated he had passed out, leaving Kevin and Brian at the helm. Andy was too small to maneuver a sailboat, but apparently not too young to sink in one.

They had started taking in water and Toni thought they were all going to die. Luckily they hadn't gone too far out and the kids managed, somehow, to get everyone back home.

Toni had always dreaded water, and that accident certainly didn't make things better.

San Antonio turned out to be a very crucial stint in the Woods' vagabond life. It was there that Toni had her first real emotional breakdown. Pushed to the limit, she felt she could no longer stay in that house. While David was at work one day, she gathered the kids, packed them in the car and drove all the way to Bremerton. David had to get special emergency leave to reach them citing spousal abandonment, a rather unusual dispensation to request in the military environment.

He picked wife and sons and up and drove back to San Antonio overnight, falling asleep on the way and ending up off the highway with various flat tires.

Luckily, no one was hurt.

San Antonio was also where Andy got his first taste of the stage. On April 9th 1976, Gerald Ford, the 38th President of the United States, in full swing of his campaign trail, was to hold a rally at the Alamo Mission, the fortress compound founded in the 18th century by Roman Catholic missionaries, now part of San Antonio's Historic District.

Andy, ten years old, announced to his mother he wanted to shake hands with the President. Toni was more than willing to take him to the rally, but she also warned him.

"You're not gonna get anywhere close to the President, darling. Don't get your heart set on that. It's gonna be a big crowd."

"Just take me to town, please", was Andy's response.

So they went. They parked a few blocks away, and as they made their way to the Alamo, they could see the stage in the distance.

When Andy spotted legendary NBC anchor Tom Brokaw and the President himself walking towards the stage, he suddenly broke away from Toni and tore through the crowd. Toni ran after him but lost sight of him in the swarm of people. Minutes later, as she wove her way through, she saw the President lean down from the stage and shake two tiny little hands. "Oh, and who is this little guy?" she heard him ask, backed by Brokaw, right before kicking in with his speech.

"At the outset, I want to thank the San Antonio Bicentennial Committee and the Daughters of the Republic of Texas..."

That little guy was Andy.

He had pushed himself all the way to the front of the stage and fulfilled his dream of shaking the President's hand.

In the weeks to come, he would cold call various San Antonio residents, trying to persuade them to vote for Ford. It was his personal political phone campaign, made by a ten year old kid for a Republican President.

Gerald Ford lost the elections to Jimmy Carter, in the end. Andy was so disappointed he decided to write Ford a letter, expressing how sorry he was.

Once again, Toni gently advised him not to expect a reply. But to everybody's surprise, a few weeks later Andy received a letter back. The former president remembered exactly who that little guy was.

Andy could see the things he needed and make them happen.

This would be one of his major talents in the years to come.

CHAPTER 4

Being like Kiss

"Andy was cherubic. If you had to squeeze his head, you had no shit coming out of it."

- Kim Thayil, Soundgarden, interviewed for Malfunkshun: The Andy Wood Story *by Scot Barbour.*

Of the three Wood brothers, Kevin had been the first to display any interest in a musical instrument, namely the violin. He was nine years old when he became fascinated with Beethoven, frequently playing on his parents' stereo. Before that, he had been fascinated with The Beatles, one of his mother's favorites, as had Brian. Not fascinated enough to imagine themselves as musicians though. Kevin's love for the violin was short-lived and he would later switch to guitar.

As for Andy, he had been a rock star since a very early age. He had written his first song at just three, while David was in Vietnam. Kevin had decided to record a tape to send to their dad, and had asked Andy to say something. Sitting in his stroller, Andy had started mumbling a tune, improvising the following lyrics:

"Baby I Love You so much/ singin' in the weeds"

No apparent meaning, but it was... a song. Kevin made a copy and sent it to David, not exactly sure it would reach him.

It did.

The kids' connection to music had deep roots in David's own love for rock. He liked Black Sabbath and Led Zeppelin, and he liked his stereo speakers to blast them out at high volumes. When he was home, David was in charge of the musical selection. At the time not every household featured a television set, so the hi-fi stereo and radio were the only sources of entertainment. But the radio didn't play rock music back then, just Top 40 stuff.

Though David had studied some French horn back in school, that would remain his only attempt at making music.

Andy on the other hand cultivated his passions with resolve. He had lots of them, keeping him busy all the time, but music came first. He projected himself into a world he could only read about in magazines. He kept journals where he diligently wrote pages and pages of questions and answers for his fake interviews. He practiced his signature hundreds of times, preparing for the autographs he would have to sign.

During his stay in San Antonio, Andy had also added one more passion to the list: the Dallas Cowboys, the storied NFL team based in Dallas-Fort Worth, Texas. Andy's obsession for the Dallas Cowboys translated into his very own fantasy football. He would make up an entire league of teams and seasons, keeping track of the scores for each game, all written down in his diaries, filled with pages of fake matches and fake results.

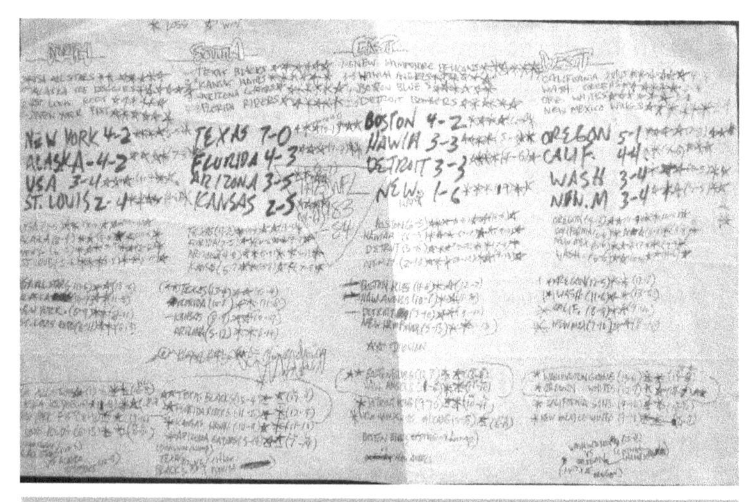

Andy's Fantasy Football.
Courtesy of Toni Wood.

At one point Andy had imagined himself as a radio DJ, the host of a rock show, just like Howard Stern. He pretended he owned a radio station and did a DJ routine, presenting songs and interviewing imaginary people.

For one day, his dream came true. One day, he and Kevin were invited to KZOK - 102.5 FM. A show called *Your Mother Wouldn't Like It* allowed listeners to act as guest DJs. Andy had sent the show a playlist of his favorite tracks, and he had been picked to present an episode. For three hours straight, from 6pm to 9pm, he hosted the show, playing a bunch of his favorite records, talking on the phone with listeners, doing little comedy sketches and chatting endlessly. He sure didn't lack confidence: Andy was definitely a guy who wanted *to be* in front of people or, at least, talk to them.

That same radio show, with some other DJ playing The Ramones, The Stooges and The New York Dolls, would later introduce a guy called Krist Novoselic, future Nirvana bass player, to punk music.

By this time Toni was begging David to quit the Air Force, as she felt she couldn't take another relocation. Every new assignment was a nightmare; she would cry for days at the prospect of being left alone in a foreign country or another brand new place. However, Toni knew that being in the US Military meant that David's life and loyalty belonged to the United States. «We didn't issue you a family, we issued you a destiny». That's what he had been told when he enrolled. So, the family would never come first.

In 1977, after endlessly shifting from continent to continent, from state to state, the Woods finally abandoned the nomadic lifestyle. Following their stay in San Antonio, Texas they relocated to Bainbridge Island, Washington, a picturesque island just 45-minutes from Seattle by ferry. At 39 years of age, David had opted out of work with a good retirement check. Vietnam alone had granted him the right to settle down.

Back then,

> Bainbridge Island was a weird place. It was a small, rural town with lots of hippies, artists and folk music pouring out of local coffee shops. With a population of 17,000 souls, it was a tranquil and beautiful place to live in, vaguely resembling Big Sur in Northern California, or Topanga Canyon in Los Angeles. Only much more wet. During the fall, magic mushrooms would sprout all over the abandoned ranches of the area. Plenty of kids would come in on the ferry from Seattle and return to the city a few hours later, with bags full of "Liberty Caps" and "Blue Bombers". To those living in Seattle, Bainbridge Island was the wild reflection of their local music scene. Seattle was the place where everybody was into Rush or Def Leppard, while Bainbridge kids were more punk and radical and identified with the Sex Pistols and Gang of Four.[1]

There were no clubs in Bainbridge, just lots of house parties, filled with kegs and pot. Teens with colorful hair and bleak views on life.

In Bainbridge, Andy started attending the Commodore Middle School. He had a very clear idea of what school was for: not studying, but hanging with friends. School was Andy's stage, the place where he could command attention, be a smartass with the girls, joke with teachers and possibly find some musically like-minded friends.

David was determined to build a traditional log house for the family to move into, not far from the home they already owned and lived in. Toni just couldn't fathom why.

As he started building, he expected cooperation; he wanted everybody in the family to drop whatever they were doing to help him in the colossal enterprise. He would be delusional.

1 This description quotes entirely a 2014 Facebook post by actor Robert Scott Crane; https://bit.ly/3C9CyrN

Andy Wood at Commodore Middle School, Bainbridge Island, 1978-1979

For the first time in her life, Toni had a job as a secretary in a real estate company, and she was very proud of it. Andy, Kevin and Brian had school, music and girls to deal with. Brian in particular was quite occupied with the latter; he would go through girlfriends like Kleenexes.

The fact that nobody helped him, paired with the realization he was no longer able to exert control over his family, made David bitter and angry. He began to loathe his wife and children and did nothing to hide it, a behavior Toni was having increasing difficulty tolerating.

In spite of the repercussions to the family dynamics, the log house in Wardwell Road played a fundamental role in the musical development of the Wood brothers. It soon turned into a rehearsal space for young and scruffy musicians of all social backgrounds, with David's stereo system as the main source of interest. By then both Kevin and Brian had embraced the electric guitar. Kevin, a freshman at Bainbridge High School, had started crafting his way into distortion pedals with the help of a guy called Greg Gunther, who had once been his flatmate in Indianola. Kevin soon discovered the bliss of never-ending guitar solos, to be performed preferably on your knees with your eyes rolled backwards. Just like your favorite consummate rock star.

In the late Seventies, Seattle was a kind of no-man's land in the Pacific Northwest. Long before Microsoft, Amazon, Starbucks and the grunge era, it was just a black hole in Washington State. Too far, too cold, too uncomfortable to reach. In a way, it was still a cowboy town, with the logging industry and Boeing - at the time the largest aerospace company in the US - fueling the local economy.

Seattle was regularly skipped during rock tours. Of course you can't claim a city is foreign to rock culture when it's Jimi Hendrix's birthplace. Hendrix crafted his talent and found fame in the UK, but grew up in Seattle's Central District and *did* actually perform in town before leaving. His song *Spanish Castle Magic* was a tribute to a very well-known dance hall in the Seattle area where he had performed at a very young age. But, again, except for Heart, Seattle's own rock sweethearts, not much had happened in the city since.

That would change on December 8th 1977, when Kiss played the Seattle Coliseum, as part of their *Love Gun Tour*. The event would leave an indelible mark on a whole generation of local musicians. At the time Kevin and Andy had developed a veneration for Paul Stanley and Ace Frehley; their stage persona, their attitude, the outrageous makeup and crazy antics. Everything about Kiss reflected their idea of *rock*. So they bought tickets for the show.

The epiphany that forged Andy's destiny, and turned him from music lover to aspiring musician, took place right there. Kiss hadn't entered the stage yet, and Cheap Trick, the opening act, were performing. At one point Andy felt a heatwave spread throughout his spine, as if possessed. He turned to his brother and declared his intentions.

"Kevin, I'm going to be a rock star."

"You know what? I wanna be a rock star too!" Kevin replied.

After Kiss, Andy no longer wanted to become a radio DJ.

He needed a crowd to look at. A club.

Or even a stadium.

CHAPTER 5

Easter of 1980

"It was an incredible period in the history of music where a community came together and it was an incredibily like-minded group of people. Almost like the Impressionists. A group of artists that formed an observation of society in a like-minded way."

- Ken Deans, former Alice In Chains co-manager

On the fifty-five minute ferry ride that separates Bainbridge Island from Seattle, one can admire the magnificence of the Puget Sound while sailing past. From the Seattle Ferry Terminal, at Pier 50, it's just a couple of minutes walk to First Avenue via Marion Street. The area between Pioneer Square and Pike Place Market was once considered a 'red zone', where drug pushers operated undisturbed in front of the X-rated movie theatre and adult bookstores.

In the early eighties, Seattle was experiencing a full-blown recession. Boeing was still the main source of employment in the area, but it still carried the scars of the "Boeing Bust", a crisis in the early seventies that had caused a massive cut in the workforce. Somebody had ironically posted a billboard between 167th Street and Pacific Highway reading:

> "Will the last person leaving SEATTLE
> turn out the lights"

A good indication of the general mood. In short, Seattle was a city everybody wanted to escape from.

In spite of the disheartening context, the music scene in the city was percolating from East to West: both the punk and metal communities had found fertile ground to grow in, respectively in the city center and the outskirts.

In Bellevue, a satellite city in the Eastside region of Seattle's metropolitan area, a small company producing operating systems for personal computers had just moved in. It was called Microsoft Inc. But at the time it was merely an irrelevant detail in terms of the financial impact on the area.

What's more noteworthy about Bellevue was Lake Hills Roller Rink, one of the few live music venues for "all ages", and not just 21 and over.

Twenty-two miles away, in Bainbridge Island, Andy and Kevin's musical activities were greatly assisted by the death of their great-grandmother, who left them a notable sum in her will.

With that money, Andy bought his first bass guitar. Not just any bass: a lilac-colored Kramer Duke, with an aluminum neck. You didn't see many of those around. Andy had never played the bass, but he thought it could be useful in composing his tunes. He had taken piano lessons in San Antonio, but as a bass player, he was basically self-taught.

Andy figured, you don't need to *know* how to play an instrument in order to play it. You *just* play.

Kevin, not to be outdone, used his great-grandmother's money to buy a magnificent Marshall amp.

Malfunkshun, Andy's and Kevin's very first band was officially formed on Easter day 1980. Even the most dysfunctional families celebrate the main holidays, and in the case of the Woods, this was done with a yearly lunch at grandma's. That day however, Andy and Kevin decided not to join the rest of the family, and stayed at home, laying the foundations of their future. That was the day they made their first demo, recorded entirely themselves. They had all the necessary tools: a double cassette ghetto blaster, a mic, an electric guitar, a lilac-colored third-hand Kramer Duke bass and skeletons of songs they had laid out here and there.

With them was a kid from the neighborhood called Dave Hunt, an aspiring drummer.

Andy, on bass, had his work cut out for him trying to accompany Kevin in his infinite guitar solos. Truth was, Andy didn't aspire to the double role of bass player and lead vocalist, he would have preferred just being the frontman. Well, not just the frontman: he wanted to be the preacher of electric and scintillating love, a guru in makeup, a master of ceremonies.

Enter David Rees, a neighbor and one of the most enthusiastic disciples of David Wood's stereo system. Rees had never touched a bass in his life, but he borrowed one from a friend and came to practice with the dedication of a model student. Knowing how to actually play an instrument was not essential at this point.

The name of the band, Malfunkshun, was Kevin's idea. To earn money he worked at a Chinese restaurant in Bainbridge, cutting up chicken. The dishwasher often displayed the message "Report: Malfunction" and it immediately struck him as a great name for a band. He already had a logo in mind too: a man in a telephone booth with the receiver held to his ear, a mushroom of smoke rising behind him like an atomic explosion; the man is reporting a malfunction, get it?

Andy wasn't convinced and proposed they shorten it to just "Malfunction", but with the word "funk", so it became "Malfunkshun". A poetic license, but also a spoof aimed at those bands who chose complicated names just to sound hip. Like Confunkshun, a renowned funk band from California who evidently thought "Confusion" would be too ordinary.

Andy was very happy to *be* in a band. It was *his* band, even if Kevin was the ringleader.

It would be genius, profane, fun. Something totally new in Bainbridge's punk scene. And in Seattle's.

The birth of Malfunkshun coincided with Andy's enrollment in Bainbridge High School. To Andy, school was still where you socialized, hooked up with girls, smoked joints and injected some light into the otherwise dreary lives of teachers and classmates alike.

And also a place to play music, when the occasion arose.

Graced with a delicate and androgynous beauty, Andy stood out from his classmates. He was open-minded, astute and didn't care for conventions. His innate comedic streak guaranteed he was always the center of attention and could win over the most reluctant of teachers and the snobbiest of classmates.

In the halls of Bainbridge High, Andy soon noticed a punk kid who seemed very sure of himself, a real city kid. His name was Regan Hägar and he was thirteen years old. Andy and Regan spent some time studying each other before they actually spoke.

Regan wasn't happy about being in Bainbridge, his world was Seattle, where he used to live with his mother and older brother. After three consecutive break-ins to their home in Ravenna, a neighborhood on the East side of the city, and following some problems Regan had had with local authorities, going as far as spending some time in juvenile detention, his mother, an only parent of two boys in 1979, had decided to relocate to Bainbridge, which seemed safer. Regan was waging his own personal protest of the move by skipping school. He would use his lunch money to take the ferry to Seattle and spend as much as four days there, couch surfing at friends', of course without permission.

To be fair, Bainbridge was even worse than Seattle in certain aspects. House parties were getting pretty wild, with kids shooting real guns in the air while tripping on acid. In Seattle on the other hand, you'd sneak into a venue for a concert, or hunker at home in front of the TV, which only offered a handful of channels unless you were rich enough to afford cable.

Regan was very well connected in Seattle's punk scene. For various years he had played drums in a band called Maggot Brains, but most of all, he punched tickets at The Showbox, one of the main clubs of the city, in downtown Seattle, just a few blocks from Pike Place Market.

The kids at the door of the venue were seen as superior beings, their position of power generating a blind kind of envy mingled with admiration. They were the ones who decided who got in and who didn't, but most importantly, who got to see the concert for free. It also wasn't uncommon for them to let people in when the venue was sold out, pocketing the cash of the non-existent tickets themselves.

The Showbox in Seattle had been an institution since the 40s. Before being converted to a bingo hall, its stage had been graced by the likes of Nat King Cole and Frank Sinatra. Decades later, in 1979, it had reopened with its original name.

Regan had worked his way up from posting concert flyers on lampposts to managing the door, which was a well-paid job with the added perks of free tickets and pot.

On the night of August 10th 1980, Devo were performing at The Showbox. Andy and Kevin were waiting in line when they spotted Regan at the door. A quick exchange of words, and they were in.

Andy really liked Regan.
He might even be the new drummer of Malfunkshun.

CHAPTER 6

Satan's Lambs

"If you don't all come to the front we're going to play the Peter Criss solo album in its entirety."

Andy Wood, on stage.

In its first incarnation, Malfunkshun was neither a punk nor a metal band. In the place of primordial growls there were clumsy riffs on distorted guitars, with a couple of hooks shouted here and there. The first defection came early on: drummer Dave Hunt had not really connected with Andy or Kevin's idea for the band; it was too weird for him. So he left Malfunkshun to join Skin Diver, another local group whose ambition was to play like Van Halen. He was promptly replaced by Regan.

The very first Malfunkshun gig took place at Strawberry Jam, a family-friendly musical event organized every year in Bainbridge Island on a hill dotted with strawberry bushes. Bassist Dave Rees provided his 1970 Buick Estate Wagon to transport their equipment, but because there was no space left on the seats, Andy and Regan rode on the roof. By the time they arrived at their destination, Andy had a buzzcut; Regan had cut his hair on the way.

Malfunkshun's debut at Strawberry Jam was a disaster. They were booed, ridiculed and had objects thrown at them by the crowd. The situation got so out of hand even Regan, who knew a thing or two about brawls, could hardly believe it. The drunk mothers and fathers of their classmates were hurling insults at them, a bunch of teenagers just trying to play music. Terrible music, but still music. Toni was among the crowd, terrified that violence might break out at any moment.

Malfunkshun only played a few tunes, all originals, no covers. Among them was *Pictures On The TV*, the only song whose lyrics were written by Kevin, while the others were all works of Andy, such as *Human God*, the story of a man who goes mad when he finds out he's God, and *Bobbie-Jo*, dedicated to a girl at Bainbridge High who Andy had a crush on.

Dave Rees, Regan Hägar, Kevin and Andy Wood, Bainbridge Island, 1981. Photo by Peter Bunce.

When events did start to escalate, and the band had to stop, Andy seized control of the situation, addressing the crowd with a message that was as placating as it was unexpected. "What's your problem people? It's love rock history in the making!", he stated into the mic with the utmost tranquility, wearing a t-shirt with a crossed-out swastika.

The crowd went silent.

The day after Strawberry Jam it was clear to everyone that Dave Rees did *not* know how to play the bass. Mustering up as much dignity as he could find, and trying to hide his embarrassment, he took leave of the band. By this point embarrassment was the leading sentiment of the whole group actually. Andy temporarily returned as the bass player, while they looked for a substitute.

Regan, disappointed by Strawberry Jam and fueled by a rebellious punk spirit, decided Bainbridge wasn't worthy of Malfunkshun: from that moment on they would only play in Seattle, where the audience was more eclectic and receptive. He had the right connections to open certain doors.

In what would be a sort-of initiation ritual, the boys assigned themselves stage names: Andy declared himself "Landrew the Lovechild", freely inspired by Landru, the tyrannical omniscient computer of *Star Trek*; Kevin first decided to call himself "Ded Springsteen", a personal tribute to his aversion for the "The Boss", and then "Kevinstein"; Regan chose "Thundarr", in homage to his Viking roots. In that period Kevin had developed an unconventional technique on the guitar: he would scratch at it with startling speed, as if in the grips of an otherworldly power. He would go around saying he was possessed by the devil, a behavior that did nothing for his social life, and was thus soon abandoned.

Andy adopted an unusual new stage look: white greasepaint covering his entire face, heavy black eyeliner surrounding his eyes, the usual lilac Kramer Duke bass slung around his shoulder and a t-shirt with the Malfunkshun logo he had designed himself.

From that moment on the band would take to the stage with spoofs and parodies of Satanic imagery: 666 turned into 333, good against evil, love against hate. The number three became a recurring element of the band's imagery.

Andy wanted to be like Paul Stanley of Kiss, it was obvious. He wanted to reap the benefits of the multitude of listening sessions of *Alive!* from his father's stereo at a volume that would make your ears bleed. But it was UK glam rock, glittery and grotesque, that truly captured his imagination. Freddie Mercury and Queen were artists he particularly admired, the album *A Night At The Opera* was a huge source of inspiration.

It was July 1st 1980 when Queen played at The Seattle Coliseum. Andy went to see them with Dave Rees, whose exit from the band had in no way compromised their friendship. Seeing Queen perform live was a dream come true for both of them. The boys got in line in the early hours of the morning with some pot and food provisions; Rees' mother had put a bag of grapes in his lunchbox, there were tons of them. After queueing for several hours, Andy shared the bag with the other kids waiting, and eventually lost track of it. Once inside the venue and with the concert well underway, as the band were nearing the end of *We Will Rock You*, Freddie Mercury walked towards the edge of the stage and grabbed hold of something «Hey, there's a fucking bag of grapes here!».

It was *that* bag[2].

After the disastrous gig at Strawberry Jam, Malfunkshun did a few more shows in the area: at the Island Community Center in Bainbridge and a few gigs at church dances in Indianola and Winslow organized by local communities. Regan however had not wavered in his intention of debuting in Seattle. And thanks to his contacts that first gig arrived: at Serbian Hall, a historical building between 15th and Columbian Way that had been the venue for marriages and dances in the Beacon Hill community, composed also of Italian immigrants, for decades.

Malfunkshun played there on March 12th 1982. Reaching the venue was a feat in itself, as none of them had a driver's license. It was an older friend who came to their rescue and drove the station wagon Rees had so kindly put

2 Dave Rees, *In It To Spin It, snippet #6*, Seeing Queen With Andrew Wood, December 2013, youtube.com/watch?v=GA2W7hz2ETQ

at their disposal, only for it to end up in an enormous pothole in the parking lot in front of Serbian Hall. That night Malfunkshun were sharing the stage with five other local bands, among whom were the much-talked about Fartz. Before their set Andy and Regan broke into the cigarette vending machine so they could throw packs to the crowd. This earned them a very enthusiastic reception.

alfunkshun, Seattle's Serbian Hall 1982
hoto: Mike Leach, bestrockphotos.com

In the early 80s Seattle wasn't very teen-friendly. It had a reputation as being progressive and welcoming to adults and small children, but teenagers – especially those belonging to a counterculture – had a pretty rough time. That's because the local underground music scene, with its strict regulations, was mainly built around the 21-and-over. Young bands mainly played in basements and backrooms, or some small and unlikely clubs, like The Strand Hotel, or Ground Zero.

The Gorilla Room, located at 610 2nd Avenue, certainly deserves a special mention. Built in the back room of a chinese restaurant, it was home to the some of the pioneering Seattle punk bands. As local historian and journalist Clark

Humphrey put it[3], "It was a homey, raunchy, delicious place, in various degrees of being trashed."

Then there were venues like the Rosco Louie and, later, the Graven Image. Founded by the pioneering local talent of Mr. Larry Reid, they were more art galleries than proper clubs, where experimental live music and visual arts blended together. At around that time, a local entrepreneur called Hugo Piottin fell into the picture. He sensed there weren't enough places in Seattle for bands to play in, so he renovated an old tavern from the Twenties and turned it into The Metropolis.

This legendary all-ages music venue helped foment Seattle's underground music scene from May 1983 to March 1984. Its defining characteristic was an enormous parachute hanging from the wall at the rear of the stage. During its very short life span, The Metropolis was much more than just a music venue; it became an epicentre for Seattle's creative youth, not just to congregate as an audience, but also to start honing their own creative abilities.

Malfunkshun played The Metropolis regularly between 1983 and 1984. They were insolent but not offensive, and were warmly received by the punk community. But there was something else that made them stand out. Up to that point the standard for bands in Seattle had not included a stage look: they performed without much attention to aesthetics. Malfunkshun on the contrary had a very strong visual impact. Andy would take to the stage with a full face of makeup thanks to the assistance of some female friends who would paint him in the dressing room. His look included various layers of greasepaint, makeup on his eyes and lips, animal print leggings, faux fur coats and the ever-present feather boa.

All things that had been unheard of in that city, in those years.

3 From his book Loser: *The Real Seattle Music Story*, Feral House, 1995.

Malfunkshun, Seattle's Gorilla Gardens, 1984. Photo by Libby Knudson

CHAPTER 7

Your band sucks

"Going to Seattle was an experience. You had to bring all your gear in, and go to the ferry, and it took forever. It was like a giant vision quest just to go and do it."

- Joe Abrams, musician, Andy's teenage friend and jamming buddy

The log house on Bainbridge's Wardwell Road played a key role in the musical development of the Wood brothers. Here, Malfunkshun was conceived; here, they recorded their first demo that fateful Easter of 1980. That would be the house they would have the fondest memories of.

At some point, the Woods had to move again, this time to a rented duplex in Rockaway Beach. This compulsive relocating was the result of a discovery David had made: buying and flipping homes was a decent source of revenue, even if it meant the family had to resort to short-term living solutions.

Relocating to Bainbridge Island was supposed to have spelled the end of their nomadic lifestyle, but David was compelled to do and undo, to always be on the move.

Of all the new neighbors in Rockaway Beach, the Crane family stood out the most. Bob Crane had been an actor of some success, having played the lead role in the TV series *Hogan's Heroes* for many years. Following his death in quite mysterious circumstances, his wife had decided to move the family away from the perils of Hollywood.

Of the three children, Robert Scott was the eldest, and like many students at Bainbridge High, he was into punk music.

Andy and Scott met for the first time one day after school, when they both got off at the same bus stop. For a while Robert had the impression Andy was following him, then he figured out they just lived a few yards away from each other. They started to talk, and Andy told him about Malfunkshun, come down from Mount Olympus to preach the message of "Love Rock". A few minutes later they were smoking a joint in the woods.

Andy and Scott were instantly friends. Each time Andy went to his place he would solemnly announce it by declaring: "Mom, I'm going over to Little Hogan's house".

Greg Gunther, Kevin's guitar teacher, also lived round the block. In his bedroom there was a Kustom amp from the early Seventies and some blindingly orange guitars he had made himself in his workshop.

Everybody seemed happy about the move to Rockaway Beach. Except for Toni.

By then the Wood brothers had become pretty notorious in Bainbridge Island. What was morally dubious to most, was mere routine for them. Every dent on the car, every hangover, every middle finger to the law was another notch on their belt, a step towards the pantheon of rock, the stuff legends are made of.

Andy, Kevin and Brian didn't have a problem with pot, they had a problem when they *didn't* have pot. The cops had it easy in Bainbridge Island. It was always the same faces, they knew 'em all by name. The three Wood brothers would regularly get searched by police with any lousy excuse. "Routine traffic stop: exit the vehicle and remove your shoes!" Once they were even handcuffed and taken to the station, only to be released an hour later.

Moving constantly from one house to another meant the divine message of Malfunkshun could be spread throughout the island: each new home became a hub for young musicians from the local punk scene, a place where they could practice, hang out, and often crash for the night.

The Woods' kitchen was always furnished with the latest appliances, such as a microwave. Regan, who had basically become part of the household, was obsessed with it: he liked to melt cheddar on toast. He also liked having access to the fridge, which was always well-stocked.

Every afternoon, after school, the boys would always jam. There wasn't much else to do; David and Toni were basically never home, so the kids could practice for hours, accompanied by a constant cycle of cheap beer and joints. Everybody there was a minor so they had to be careful about David, who would get furious when he caught them. At the slightest hint he might be back they'd run out the back door, disappearing into the woods.

David was able to spread instant panic among the kids. Not Toni, she was more tolerant, and happy to have the house sprawling with teen spirit. More importantly, she had nothing against Andy and Regan's dalliance with makeup and teased hair. David couldn't stand it.

What Toni would hear when she'd go to the basement to do laundry though, was definitely *not* music. It was the sound of instruments being tortured, and at a volume that could make the walls crack.

The neighbors also weren't impressed. Often the Woods would find anonymous messages in their mailbox that left little room for interpretation.

"Your band sucks and isn't getting any better. Please stop."

In spite of this, the house was always open to guests. Sometimes Andy would pick them up from Eagle Harbor with his little rowboat. When they crashed on the sofa, he'd play the perfect host in the morning and prepare breakfast, his specialty was "Pancake surprise".

What the surprise was, is still unknown to these days.

There was also a fair share of girls in the Woods' house. One of the most constant presences was Whitney, Brian's girlfriend. Toni couldn't stand always finding her "big fat ass" draped over the sofa when she returned from work.

Kevin also had a girlfriend: Bonnie. It was serious. She had long, red hair and would later break his heart. That's when Kevin started drinking more heavily.

Andy was a lady's man. He certainly didn't look the part, but girls were crazy about him. A few of them helped him transform into Landrew, doing his makeup before shows.

Of all the girls that were buzzing around him there was one who was special. Her name was Mara West and she too lived in Bainbridge Island and came from a dysfunctional family. Mara was stunningly beautiful, with a porcelain complexion and striking ice-blue eyes. Most of all, she had been a fan of Malfunkshun since day one.

Andy and Mara would spend hours talking and laughing on the phone. It could have been love, but it wasn't. It didn't hurt enough.

Recreational activities in Bainbridge Island revolved around house parties. The most popular was organized by a local band called March of Crimes, an influential name in the local punk scene. No fixed location: each month it was in a different house. There would be a call to arms to all the musicians of the area and they'd play until the early hours of the morning, sustained by gallons of beer and various narcotic substances.

The lead singer of March of Crimes, Jonathan Evison[4], also went to Bainbridge High and was a few years younger than Andy and Regan, who he looked up to. They had immediately welcomed him in their circle, without any of the hazing that so often accompanies young initiates, and encouraged him to write his songs.

4 Jonathan Evison went on to be a world famous writer. His third novel, The Fundamentals Of Caring, was turned into a film by director Rob Burnett of Worldwide Pants, and released as a Netflix original in 2016.

Later, when the Woods moved to Miller Road, Andy and Jonathan became neighbors. A gravel pit halfway between their homes became the designated spot where they would smoke pot and listen to Elton John without anybody knowing and, in the evenings, they would often take the same ferry to attend gigs in Seattle.

Most of the kids orbiting around the punk scene in Bainbridge Island came from dysfunctional families. They were the ones who got beat up at school for wearing the wrong kind of pants, or for saying a word too many against a 'rival' group.

These were kids who gave their parents many a restless night: they were wild, radically punk. A life made of parties, streets, music shared with sweaty strangers, wherever, every single weekend.

March Of Crimes had two guitarists in their lineup: Ben Shepherd, a punk fundamentalist who was born in Japan and had moved to the Pacific Northwest at a very young age, and Stone Carpenter Gossard, who came from a wealthy family and lived in Seattle, but was often in Bainbridge.

Stone was a lanky kid with long hair and a prominent nose, a sharp wit and perfect comedic timing, honed from years of theatre at school. He had a natural talent for pushing people's buttons; he could identify exactly what someone's weak spot was and pound at it until they were exasperated.

Stone attended Seattle's Northwest School of the Arts, another hotbed of musical talent in the city.

One afternoon in 1983, Andy and Jonathan found themselves in the same home economics class. They decided to hang out after school and that was when Jonathan introduced Andy to Stone.

This would be a life-changing event with repercussions in the years to come.

Landrew: "In this world of sad old men-can you find a friend
Theres supposed to be something up above- spread the words of love"
-From"the Words of Love"
-Malfunkshun 1983

Regan: WAtch out for pigs!

FOR INFORMATION ON MALFUNKSHUN WRITE:
P.O. Box 10392
Bainbridge Island, WA., 98110
thanx much.

. look For Malfunkshun appearing in June with whipping boy in Seattle.

MALFUNKSHUN

*HOW LONG HAVE YOU GUYS BEEN A BAND?

Landrew: On Easter we celebrated the 2nd year of 'M-Funk". So every Easter i our birthday which we celebrate by candlelight and fruit cocktail and other fun things of that nature.

Regan: I joined the band in August of 81!to help them put out a 45 disc but that never happened and i never left!

*I COULDNT HELP BUT NOTICE ONE OF YOUR FLIERS SAID "MALFUNKSHUN RETURNS", WHY?

Landrew: Well the thing is the flier you saw was for the show that was supposed to be today(5/13/83) but was cancelled for undisclosed reasons-and the showwas in Seattle in a place that we havent played since we opened for Disch last year-so it really was to be "Malfunkshuns Return"!!

*WHEN ARE YOU EXPECTING THE DEMO OUT?

Landrew: Everybody who has ordered the demo tape and everybody who is going to get them anyway should be receiving the stuff in the mail by early June-we are very sorry for the delay its been quite a long wait and we wanted to be sure to make it worth the wait.

*IF YOU COULD OPEN FOR ANY BAND WHO WOULD IT BE? WHY?

Landrew: I really couldnt answer that question cause there are so many bands that would be great to play with- i mean of course it would be a band that attracted a lot of people but when you say that you begi- to dream. We'll play most anywhere with most anybody as long as the police dont come and stop us-we've done just about that too. We've opened for jazz bands and folk bands and Irish sing'ng groups- and then there was Discharge and of course th late great Fartz.... we're young and willing".....

Regan: Queen.

*WHATS THE BEST SHOW YOU EVER SAW?

Landrew: I dont mean to sound like Mr.Proud but it was us in a dream...I saw Malfunkshun in a dream...we were in control and the crowd was in a state of complete chaos (hint, hint) and- another great show was the Dallas Cowboys beating the Denver Broncos in the Superbowl in 1978.

Regan: Discharge and Public Image!

*WHAT ARE YOU GOING TO NAME YOUR DEMO TAPE?

Landrew: We have played around with titles but we dont think it needs to be called anything but what it is-MALFUNKSHUN!!!

Regan: In my mind I named it (Side 3) and I put it on some we mailed!

*HAVE YOU HEARD ANYTHING ABOUT THE MEAT PUPPETS GIG?

Landrew: I dont do much fishing myself (haha) I wish I did we'd love to meet the meat! (ha ha)

Regan: We should not speak of such things for it is bad karma.

*WHAT GOALS HAVE YOU SET FOR MALFUNKSHUN?

Landrew: Goals, weve got our eyes on the top! I feel we have something to off to the whole music world-the whole entertainment world! Right now, as i've s before, we're just beginning we are still in our fetal stages- we play wild, loud, Rock-N-Roll music. But in reality we have so much more to offer- We're no"wallet in the back pocket band"-we want to put on a show for the people th come to see us we want people to put aside their prejudice and put aside ther serious anti-fun attitudes and come along. We plan to begin a Dynasty-if you will-we want the stars and when we get them we want staying power...

Malfunkshun interview printed in Simplex 1 fanzine, issue #3, June 1983. Published/edited by Jonathan Evison.
Courtesy of Rod Moody / Pacific Northwest Archive

CHAPTER 8

Have three jobs. One is your band.

"He'd go to the Central Tavern when there were like 25 people there and play it like it was a coliseum. He'd be like,'To all you people in the back!' and [the only person back there] was the guy at the door."

- Mike McCready, Pearl Jam Twenty, Cameron Crowe, 2011

In the mid eighties the predominant idea in Seattle's music community could be outlined as follows: if you were from New York, Minneapolis or Athens, you were

Bainbridge High School "Talent Show", Stephen Nelson, Joe Abrams, Andrew Wood, 1984. Courtesy of Eric Petring

undoubtedly going to be a more successful musician than anyone from Seattle. If you were from Los Angeles, bingo: more record deals, more hairspray, more rock 'n' roll, baby. No surprise that Jimi Hendrix, who grew up in Seattle's Central District, had moved to California (and later the UK) to hone his damn talent.

Though it was true that most bands in Seattle played mainly for the glory, it was also true that some were able to make as much as two hundred dollars a night, a considerable sum for the time. Ten Minute Warning, probably the best hardcore punk band in Seattle then, was one of these.

The group included Greg Gilmore, considered the best drummer in town, and guitarist/bassist Andrew McKagan, later known as 'Duff'.

Raised with seven other siblings in a family of little means, Duff always sported a leather jacket and a perfectly shaped mohawk. He was shy and kind, but with big dreams of success. He soon left Seattle for Los Angeles, with just a few rags to his name and a liver already worn out from excessive alcohol consumption.

He had answered an ad in the paper by a guy named 'Slash', who was hiring musicians for his new band. That band would be Guns N' Roses, and Duff would permanently stay in LA.

Andy was good friends with Duff; they had met one night at The Grey Door, one of the few blessed sinister clubs in Pioneer Square, that was frequented by the artistic avant-garde.

It wasn't uncommon for bands to spend the night there after their performance: it was one of those places that also served as a hostel for musicians.

The good thing about the Seattle local scene was the healthy, voracious competition that fueled bands whose sound was completely different, yet had the same authentic and dirty quality. That gritty roar that came from the two sides of the city – the Eastside and the Westside – and clashed on school grounds, in the streets, in small and unlikely clubs that disappeared as quickly as they had appeared.

The Eastside was dominated by the heavy metal community, where there was a strong line separating bands from their public: fans idolized musicians like divinities, considered unreachable and untouchable. On the Westside on the other hand, dominated by the punk community, bands regularly socialized with their fans. No backstage adoration.

At some point punks started crossing over Lake Washington to check out what was happening on "the other side". And when the two scenes met, it would often end in an ugly fight, especially if the BoPoBoys were involved.

The BoPos were basically a gang of thugs, classic leather punks whose idea of fun was to crash a party uninvited and get into a fight, and maybe trash the TV. They fit into the punk-noise thing that was happening and they would look for trouble with everyone and everywhere.

Seattle was an effervescent microcosm in which musicians would meet and study each other. Most musicians lived and worked with other musicians, and inevitably, they had a day job too. The motto was "Have three jobs, one of which is your band", so some washed dishes, some deboned chickens, others delivered for FedEx. All occupations that were never mentioned in conversation, because the *real* job was music. Which is why the day job had to be flexible, something that allowed them to take days off if they had to go on tour or record an album. In the best of cases.

The common denominator of all the bands was a kind of black humor that can only be bred from boredom and an acute awareness that nobody – truly nobody – was coming from L.A. to offer them a record deal. And nobody, excluding friends and relatives, cared about their music.

There was bleak sarcasm but also self-deprecating humor and biting satire, the kind that drove bands such as the

Limp Richerds to write a song like *Death to Ivar*. Ivar's was a local institution: a renowned and long-running chain of restaurants that specialized in seafood. The lyrics went

"Death To Ivar / He's a mean, mean man / he violates clams / I don't care if he sponsored Monty Python[5] */ I wanna see him deep fat fried."*

In general, if you wanted to make a living from music, Seattle was a city you wanted to run away from. Well, unless you were Jeffrey Allen Ament, a 20-year old from Big Sandy, Montana. He deliberately *chose* to live in Seattle.

Jeff's father was a barber and had been the Mayor of Big Sandy; a double sentence for Jeff, because it meant he was expected to have exemplary conduct, as the son of the mayor, and impeccable, very short hair, as the son of the barber[6].

He was a skateboarder, and had been accepted to the University of Montana, in Missoula, where he planned to pursue his passion for graphic design.

It was the same college attended by Bruce Fairweather, a tall and outgoing guy from Honolulu.

Among a number of Universities, he had picked the University of Montana following a thorough examination of the college's informative pamphlet, which had provided a decisive element. The campus had brick banks the kids could skate on. This was enough for Bruce to make the final decision. "There, I want to go there", he'd told his parents.

It was on those banks, the first day of college, that Jeff and Bruce met and became friends. For the first time in their lives, they felt surrounded by their own tribe: dozens of punk skaters in shorts and Sex Pistols t-shirts.

It was heaven on earth.

5 The reference to *Monty Python* was because the chain's founder, Ivar Haglund, had financed the airing of cult series Monty Python's Flying Circus on local channel KCTS-TV.

6 *Chat With Jeff Ament*, ESPN Sportsnation, espn.go.com/sportsnation/chat/_/id/23827, December 2014

A few months later, returning from Christmas break, Jeff and Bruce formed a hardcore punk band called Deranged Diction, where Jeff played bass, an instrument that was completely unknown to him at that point. Not long thereafter they both dropped out of college to dedicate themselves completely to music and, by the Summer of 1982, Jeff had decided to move to Seattle. He loaded his car with his skateboard, a few suitcases, two hundred dollars for gas and drove off, away from a family that was loving but "hardcore catholic", as he described them.

Bruce would join him not much later.

CHAPTER 9

SEPARATE LIVES

"One time I saw Malfunkshun in Olympia, and there's about fifty people there and they are all standing in the back watching them and I put up a chair right in front of the stage and I sat there and fell asleep and Andrew Wood was like singing to me the whole night and making fun of me and dancing around me. I felt like I healed when I woke up."

Kurt Cobain, MTV News, 1992

Toni certainly had no intention of divorcing, as she left the house in Rockaway Beach.

It was supposed to be a dramatic gesture, carried out in a moment of exasperation. What had started as a fight like many others however, had reached a point of no return.

Tension in the Woods' household could be cut with a knife. It got exacerbated by the fact that no one in the family was sober anymore. Everybody was either drunk or high, and Toni had no one to talk to[7]. Often, when everybody had left slamming the doors behind them, Brian would be the only one to come slowly back into the kitchen. "C'mon mom, let's do the dishes", he would say.

---

7 This description is taken from an interview with Toni Wood from the documentary *Malfunkshun: the Andy Wood Story*, by Scot Barbour (2005). Kevin Wood, in the course of an interview with the author of this book, disputed this version of events, maintaining his mother was conditioned by the huge stress of Andy's death. Kevin stated: "We were a very close-knit family. We had our ups and downs. We were born into the military environment, where the use of alcohol is very prevalent. The frictions we experienced as young adults were no more no less than everybody did. We had a wonderful childhood."

What had been cracks in Toni's relationship with David were now irreparable fractures. They hurt each other constantly, both emotionally and physically. One day, there had been one fight too many, one slammed door too many, Brian had returned drunk one time too many. So, Toni had grabbed an enormous bag and stuffed it with a pillow, a toothbrush, a few other things, and had rented a room in a cottage nearby.

David had started stalking her out every day on the road to the cottage when she came back from work, trying to win her back.

But it didn't work.

Toni had made up her mind.

But she never said the word "divorce".

One day David showed up with some papers. "Just sign here", he ordered. And Toni signed, without giving it a second thought.

They were divorce papers.

David's resentment was perfectly distilled in a small clause concerning surviving spouse pension.

From that moment on, the two of them led separate lives. David moved into a house a few minutes by car from Rockaway Beach. The property came with a small cottage that Kevin rented together with Andy.

It was Brian who took the divorce the hardest. For various weeks he roughed it on the streets of Seattle, sleeping outside stores in Capitol Hill.

Toni rented a small apartment in a very old and very beautiful house on Sunrise Drive, named this way because of the breathtaking sunrises that occur on certain winter days.

At that point Toni was the bad guy. She was the one responsible for breaking up the happy family while David was the victim and could rely on his sons' sympathy. One day he asked the boys to take him to her apartment while she was out. Once inside, he collapsed on the floor next to the chimney and started crying his eyes out. "No matter where she lives she just makes it a home, doesn't she?", he moaned.

For a while Toni was on the outside looking in when it came to the lives of her boys. She felt guilty and couldn't bring herself to broach the subject with them. Andy, fourteen at the time, suffered from the divorce, but he never really pushed his mother away. He did feel like he was living a surreal version of his favorite Glen Campbell song, *You Better Sit Down Kids*, sung from the point of view of a dad explaining to his kids that he's separating from their mother and moving out.

Despite the turmoil, Andy adapted quickly to the new family setting, and started going to Toni's house almost everyday after school. Sometimes, she would be at work, so he would just sit down on the floor by himself and go through her mom's records, pick one at random and listen to it. Just like he used to do when they all lived together.

Andy had a remarkable gift for making the best of any given situation, and even his mom's empty house didn't inhibit that ability.

One day he came across a bossanova LP and put it on the turntable. The song that started playing was an instrumental. Since nobody was singing, Andy started to: he improvised lyrics about love and recorded himself on a tape he later gave to his mother. He told her it was a bossanova love song for her, the title was *Landrew For Mom*.

Soon after, Toni was sipping a drink in a café in Bainbridge when she remembered she had the tape in her bag. She hadn't listened to it yet so she asked the barista if he could play it on the PA system. The café was soon permeated with Andy's sweet lyrics over a smooth Bossanova beat. Gradually, Andy's voice started rising in volume, intensity and use of profanity, until it was a series of unintelligible grunts worthy of the worst punk bands. The tape had been a joke. But the café had gone quiet.

Promotional MFunk poster by Loosegroove Records.

Even after the divorce, Toni kept going to Malfunkshun gigs. She had started working in a retirement home and had to get up very early in the morning, but it didn't matter: she liked seeing her boys cut their teeth in the music industry, even if it was in the worst dumps of Seattle.

She usually left before the end of their set, catching the 11:10pm ferry back to Bainbridge.

When Toni arrived at a venue Andy always made sure she made a grand entrance: «A chair for the lady, please», he'd imperially announce. And someone from the audience would always pull a chair out for her. An audience of twenty people, at best.

What Andy and Kevin were doing at those shabby makeshift clubs wasn't just jamming with friends, they were forging their talent. Toni noticed Andy oozed charisma, he was born to be on stage. But he lacked substance. She encouraged him not just to play the part of the consummate rock star, but also to deliver a message. "If people start listening to you, you'd better have something to say", she told him.

Andy loved interacting with the audience, especially the kids that were holding up the wall like it depended on them for stability. "If you're just gonna stand there, why don't you go sit at the bar?", he would enquire. He was bold, but he lacked structure. This applied to his songs too: it was clear how they started, but nobody knew when they ended. Andy and Regan would try to signal the conclusion of a song with a jump, a gesture, an exchange of looks. But Kevin always continued with a guitar solo that could last as long as ten minutes, until it segued directly into the next song.

What was clear though, was that Malfunkshun was different from all other bands. Grotesque, ironic, excessive: a unique blend of metal and glam rock. A band come down from Mount Olympus to spread the message of universal love. No relation to the Greek divinities, of which none of the band members had the least notion.

Their Mount Olympus was no more no less the majestic mountain in western Washington state.

1 (WE ARE) SATAN'S LAMBS (A. WOOD K. WOOD R. HAGAR)
2 KILL OR BE KILLED (ON THE BATTLEFIELD) (K. WOOD)
3 WORDZ OF LOVE (A. WOOD)
4 YOUNG AND WILLING (A. WOOD K. WOOD R. HAGAR)
5 ROCK-N-ROLL LOVER (A. WOOD K. WOOD)
6 AGGRESSOR (A. WOOD K. WOOD R. HAGAR)
7 CHAMPION (A. WOOD R. HAGAR K. WOOD)
8 SHE'S GONE (K. WOOD)
9 PRETTY MODERN BOYZ (A. WOOD)
10 WOMBAT (I AM THE) (A. WOOD)
11 ANSWER TO THE PRAYERS (A. WOOD K. WOOD)
12 PICTURES ON THE T.V. (K. WOOD)
13 LITTLE RED ROOSTER (A. WOOD)
14 NO, NO, NANETTE (A. WOOD)
15 ~~POOR, POOR, CHILDREN (A. WOOD, K. WOOD, R. WOOD)~~
16 THE MALFUNKSHUN (A. WOOD K. WOOD)
17 MY LOVE (Rest in my arms…..) (A. WOOD)
18 SEX MACHINE (A. WOOD)
19 SMEGMA HOUND (A. WOOD K. WOOD)
20
21
22
23
24

NEW

the tracklist for one of the various Malfunkshun home-recorded demo tapes.

CHAPTER 10

STREAKS OF MASCARA DOWN MY FACE

"My senorita dances for me
Complete with vaseline and a jar of LSD
My little doggie she barks all night
And no I've never owned a woman
Because you can't own women."

- Andy Wood, Mr Liberty (With Morals)

One winter night in 1983, Malfunkshun were booked for a live set at the legendary Blue Moon Tavern, in Seattle's University District. The Blue Moon was one of Seattle's first legal bars following the end of Prohibition. It's what the locals call "a hole-in-the-wall" bar, where pushers, hookers, punks and local residents blend seamlessly. Quoting local novelist James Knisely: "It's a proper dive. And not just murky, sticky, and dense: it's ugly. Ugly to the studs. It's beautiful."

What was supposed to be a Malfunkshun gig turned into a solo performance by Andy. For some reason, Regan and Kevin didn't show up, leaving him alone as master of ceremonies, with his keyboard, his white face and his pink jacket. Despite his flamboyance, Andy had always been reluctant to perform solo, so the gig really pushed him out of his comfort zone. That night was memorable, especially to Toni. She was in the audience – a total of about twenty people, displaying various degrees of indifference. When the time came for her to leave so she could catch the ferry to Bainbridge, Andy interrupted his performance.

"Excuse me people" he announced on the mic, "I'm going to walk my mom to the car. I'll be right back."

As she kissed him goodbye in the parking lot, Toni noticed streaks of tears streaming down Andy's face, over his thick white make-up and dripping on his pink jacket.

"What's the matter, honey?", she asked. "Oh, don't worry. Just go or you'll miss your ferry", he replied promptly, smiling and crying simultaneously. Toni would never forget that moment. She had never seen Andy break down in that way.

Andy had started smoking pot at a very young age, like many other kids. He soon indulged in other recreational drugs, namely acids and magic mushrooms. Toni didn't seem too concerned; every single man in her life up to that point had either been an alcoholic or a drug user, only the substance changed. In the army environment you were a freak if you weren't a heavy drinker, anything less than that was frowned upon and highly suspicious. So, when her kids had started doing drugs, Toni had assumed it was a rite of passage. She had no idea how wrong she was.

By then, Andy had become a very prolific songwriter. His lyrics were inspired by life itself; everyday, ordinary life. Every little meaningless and mundane event became precious material for a new song. Andy was capable of turning the most banal incident into dramatic, theatrical verses. The dog didn't *just* have fleas. The dog was infested by tiny, bloodthirsty creatures from hell coming to suck his soul dry and leave behind just a pile of bones and fur. Toni was convinced Andy could have written lyrics about a toilet brush if he had wanted to. The song *My Only Fan* is a clear example of Andy's sense of catastrophe mixed with wry humor. It tells the compelling drama of a friend whose only fan, in the sense of an air circulator, breaks on the hottest day of the year.

Andy's biggest source of inspiration for his lyrics though, was love. A tormented and tortured kind of love in all its tragic outcomes. Years of exposure to his parents' toxic relationship had distilled a very clear idea of what love looked like; Andy grew up knowing that true love had to hurt. That was the hard truth he sang in his songs, and it was the vicious cycle he spiralled down in his own relationships.

His song *Mr.Liberty (With Morals)*[8] can be interpreted as a manifesto for his own approach to relationships and sex.

8 *Mr Liberty (With Morals)* is featured on *Return To Olympus*, the only

Free love, but with ethics.For love, Andy once even put his friendship with Regan on the line. It was because of a girl at school, whom Andy liked and who liked him back. But he was too shy to make a move, so eventually she turned her attention to Regan, and ended up becoming *his* girlfriend. Andy was crushed; it almost drove a wedge between them. They spent hours in a log cabin, fighting and crying and eventually hugging it out and apologizing to each other. Regan hadn't realized how much he had hurt Andy, so it became a real bonding moment for them. It was unusual for two boys of fourteen and fifteen to cry and discuss their emotions so openly, when the slightest hint of weakness was enough to get bullied and beat up at school.

Andy got bullied a lot. Kids who wore make-up and their mother's lingerie were easy targets for gangs like the BoPo Boys. One kid in particular named McClark constantly targeted Andy, and beat the shit out of him at parties. Regan got bullied a lot too, because of his androgynous look, but he always responded and wasn't afraid to look the Boys in the eye. While Andy was scared shitless, and that just made it worse. The fact that he was bullied in no way undermined an indisputable truth: Andy was much loved at school, because he embraced the outsiders. Both him and Regan defended gay kids from bullies. They knew who they were, even though they hadn't come out. The fact, there was no way they could come out, as they would have had to leave school. But Andy and Regan always gave a nod to them when passing in the hallway, as if to say «We are with you. You are welcome in our group. Welcome to drink or smoke with us». People with a handicap, be it physical or mental, they were safe with Andy and Regan.

In general, Andy and Regan championed the outcasts, as they felt like ones in the first place. Teachers couldn't bring themselves to be too strict with him though, he was just too charming. «He doesn't want to work, he just wants to *visit*», they would say.

---

album by Malfunkshun, released by Loosegroove Records in 1995. Loosegrove is a Seattle-based record label formed by Pearl Jam guitarist Stone Gossard and Regan Hagar in 1994. Initially a subsidiary of Sony it went independent in 1996.

At Bainbridge High, Andy was in the so-called "resource room", a separate, remedial classroom where students with learning disabilities are given academic assistance. One of the teachers once made a confession to Toni. "Between you and me, Andy is the smartest kid I ever taught in my life." David had always been very strict about grades and discipline. He stubbornly dragged his son towards the goal of graduation, checking on him constantly, meeting teachers, making sure he attended. For all his faults, David had a noble objective: he wanted his kids to have an education.

On June 8th 1984, Andy woke up in his bed, early in the morning. For a moment he thought it would be just another day, but it wasn't. It was the *last* day of school. The final day of a three-day graduation ceremony with its hideous dress code. The final stretch, and his time at Bainbridge High would be history.

Andy's last assignment at Bainbridge High School had been an essay: "In detail, according to a calendar, after considerable thought – give me a week by week account of what you're planning to do this summer. Begin the assignment with a set of goals you are going to accomplish. Depending on the length, severity and sincerity of the assignment, it may be the only work that you will have to complete». He ended his assignment with the following:

"(..) I don't however feel any pride in wearing a silly hat and gown in front a bunch of people wholl [sic] look at me and smile and not realize what I did was really noteworthy. Their kids are all going off to college with their 3.5 and 4.0 grade points and I graduated by the stripes of my teeth. I've never felt like part of their world and I don't want to join it now. It's a very hard position for me to be in".
(...)
"I want out of the house I now live in...I want first of all with graduation money, which may or may not exist, to find a place either here or in Seattle that me and Denise (if she can play her role) and anyone else can get into".

Denise was the girl Andy was dating at the time. She was right there, at the graduation ceremony.

She was the one who introduced Andy to heroin.

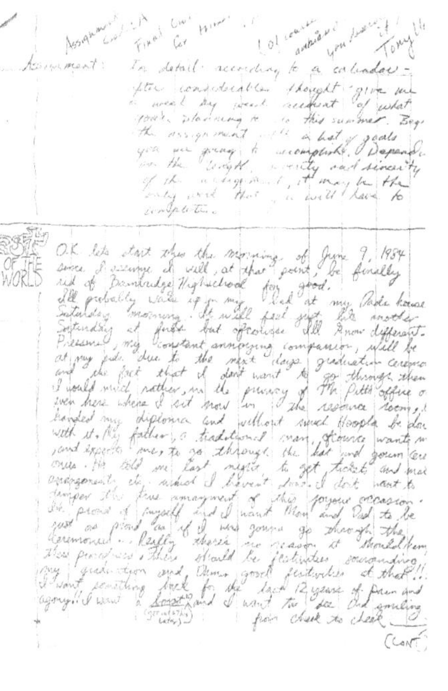

Assignment [illegible] Final [illegible] for [illegible] Lol [illegible] [illegible] you [illegible] it! Tony!!

Assignment: In detail, according to a calendar — after considerable thought give me a week by week account of what you're planning to do this summer. Begin the assignment with a list of goals you are going to accomplish. Depending on the length, [illegible] and sincerity of the assignment, it may be the only work that you will have to [illegible] completion.

O.K. lets start thru the morning of June 9, 1984 since I assume I will, at that point, be finally rid of Bainbridge Highschool for good.
I'll probably wake up in my bed at my Dad's house Saturday morning. It will feel just like another Saturday at first but ofcourse I'll know different. Pressure, my constant annoying companion, will be at my side due to the next days graduation ceremony and the fact that I don't want to go through them. I would much rather, in the privacy of Mr. Pitt's office or even here where I sit now in the resource room, be handed my diploma and without much Hoopla be done with it. My father, a traditional man, ofcourse wants me, and expects me, to go through the hat and gown ceremonies. He told me last night to get tickets and make arrangements etc. which I haven't done. I don't want to dampen the true amazement of this joyous occasion. I'm proud of myself and I want Mom and Dad to be just as proud as if I was gonna go through the ceremonies... Really there's no reason it should harm these proceedings. There should be festivities surrounding my graduation and damn good festivities at that!! I want something back for the last 12 years of pain and agony!! I want a Toast (get into this later) and I want to see Dad smiling from cheek to cheek.
(CONT)

because all of his millions of lectures and all his countless meetings w/ teachers and all the strife I put him through has finally paid off... Once there was no light and now I have reached the end of the tunnel. I'm amazing myself as I write this and realize what a hard long journey it's been. Mr. Pitts, as you well know, recently called me the "the success story of BHS." I am, once again, Damn proud (!!!) of the comeback victory I accomplished!!! I don't however feel any pride in wearing a silly hat and gown in front of a bunch of people who'll look at me, smile and not realize what I did was really noteworthy. These kids are all going off to college with their 3.5 and 4.0 gradepoints and I graduated by the skin of my teeth. I've never felt like part of their world and I don't want to join it now... It's a very hard position for me to be in.
Everything is so "iffy" and sketchy at this point I really can't write exactly what I will be doing here in the beginning of my real life. I can, however, tell you what I want to do and what I am working towards. I want out of the house I now live in.... I want to first of all, with graduation money, which may or may not exist, to find a place either here or in Seattle that me and Denise (if she can play her role) and anyone else can get into. I must [illegible] then find a state of permanent job to my liking to continue to pay my rent on a monthly basis. Our plan was for me and my brother [illegible] to get a house with a [illegible] for band rehearsal. [illegible] was also a part of this plan but to my [illegible] he tells me he couldn't live w/ me anymore (broke my heart the [illegible]). So yes, I'm gonna get a job, I'm gonna get the car my Dad left me use [illegible] for. It is a necessity as a drivers license is a nearby plan of action for me. I look forward to this life happening. I don't expect it to be given to me but that's what I meant by a Toast. It's really bogus that after all of the →
(24 hrs. later)

strain I've gone through, and all the [illegible] kissing I've had to do to get a damn diploma now that I'm gonna get one I still won't be able to get what I want. They might even make me stay until Tuesday the 12th I found out today. I don't want a cake and ice cream or even a California Cooler party when I'm done if that's all I'm gonna get. I don't mean to sound like an ass but I'm just really mad as hell about it all. I can't expect my parents and relatives to dole out mega bucks for me especially when I know my mom doesn't have it and I've either ruined or lost nearly $900.00 worth of stuff of my Dad's in the last few weeks. People think I'm gonna be a bum all these college bound ex-friends of mine think I'm not even graduating and that I'll never be anything in life. Well more school after 12 years sure doesn't sound like very much fun to me!! And there's nothing I want to be except for a musical entertainment artist, and that's it. I am willing to play bars for years until I and my friends begin to enter the major leagues of Rock and Roll.. We really haven't ever made a dent in the minors yet and still we have some pretty impressive claims to fame under our belt.. I'm convinced I'm gonna be famous in some way shape or form that's all there is to it. And in order to please those who ask "and what if you don't?" I offer this: If I never quite reach the top of the rock pile or even somewhere on the rockpile I will, as anyone with self respect would, find my peace of mind elsewhere and that will be my problem if the time comes. I highly doubt I'll become a heroine addict and die in the gutter — somewhere.. I've never liked booze enough to become an alcoholic and I don't want to get a haircut (just thought I might as [illegible] that in while I could).

"You know the saying that actors and the like say when they are accepting awards "I'd like to thank all the little people on the way who helped me...." Well you know years from now when I win some kind of award of merit for my activities I'll think back and you Ms. [illegible] still won't be just a "little person". Without the help you gave me when "chips were down"

(CONT.)

I would not be here right now and you know that's true. Me and my Dad were talking last night about what we should get you as a token of our appreciation / So what do you know??

(Hrs. later) Here's some balloons!!!! and another token of joyous graduational bliss are coming on Sunday. I'm not very good at saying thanks when I really mean it.. It's alot easier to write. Well anyway with all the pressure on me right now about getting a job and getting (believe it or not) a haircut of all things(!!!) I'm pretty tense right now. Me and Denise had a completely irrefutable argument/fight combo last night as an example. Again, well anyway as I sit in a desk in a room I will never sit in again I begin once again to realize that it's real, it's graduation.. I'm hitting the highway and I'm entering the new horizon of tomorrow.. I am venturing into the oblivion of responsibility.. I am traveling upstream with hardly a paddle to row with. I hear there's a job at the [illegible] Cafe downtown and I'd love to jump on that one.. I won't quit, I'm anxious to prove everybody wrong and make up all their narrow minds when I'm staring at them in their Sunday paper!! The hair stays!!! The look stays!!! The Rock n Roll stays and Andrew Patrick Wood will take on the world!!!! and win!!!!!!!

From the day I threatened to beat the windows out of your car to this day when I present to you (and Mrs. Green, [illegible] and Corine) a bouquet of balloons of all things!!!! It's been a time I will remember always and even when our ships are in distant seas I will think you in my mind. For some reason I am reminded of the scene in the "Wizard of Oz" where Dorothy is just about ready to say goodbye to the Scarecrow and Tinman and Lion.. It's a sad goodbye but we shall always keep in touch. Stay on the brightside dudes and always have a goodone —

Andrew Wood ☆ ☆ ☆ 6/8/84

(CONT.)

Andy's final assignment at Bainbridge High School, 06/08/1984 Courtesy of Toni Wood

PART 2

CHAPTER 11

A KILLER BAND

"Recognition [for Malfunkshun] never came enough. We always were confused by that. Bruce Pavitt of Sub Pop would never write about us in The Rocket magazine. And we had been in town for years playing big gigs, opening up for Discharge at the Showbox, we impacted a lot of these people who are now succesful, we rocked them, we made them change their minds about what they could do and what music could be."

- Regan Hägar, Interview with the author, 2015

Gary Leon Ridgway: a name that will ring a bell even to those not familiar with the Pacific Northwest.

It was the name of the man known as 'The Green River Killer', the country's deadliest convicted serial killer, who claimed to have murdered at least eighty women, mainly sex workers and runaways, between 1982 and 2003, the year of his arrest. He would strangle them and dump their bodies like bags of trash in the Green River (hence the nickname) or in remote wooded areas.

Given those circumstances, calling a Seattle punk band *Green River* in the early eighties was definitely a slap in the face to the community's sense of decency. That certainly wasn't a deterrent to Marc McLaughlin, known as Mark Arm, a novice musician but an institution of the city's punk circuit.

Known for his biting sarcasm and an approach to the stage that was destructive to say the least, (and freely inspired by Iggy Pop), Arm was the frontman of Mr. Epp and The Calculations, in his own words "the worst band in Seattle". But his credibility in the punk scene was mostly established through his collaboration with local fanzine *Attack*, where he reviewed records.

If there was one character who best embodied the madness and dark humor that permeated Seattle in those years, it was Mark Arm.

Green River were officially born one night in 1984 at the Metropolis. On that night, Jeff Ament, bass player for Deranged Diction, was in the booth playing records. Jeff had long been on Mark's radar: he desperately wanted him to join Mr. Epp, but Jeff had declined; they were the worst band in Seattle after all.

On that night, though, Mark and Jeff ended up spending hours discussing which track of Aerosmith's *Rocks* album was the best, and from that moment on they were friends, and the band was formed shortly thereafter.

From a musical standpoint, Green River were like a weird blend of Black Sabbath and The Stooges, to whom they paid tribute and parodied in equal measure. During their performances they were uncontainable: Mark Arm attacked the stage, he would devour it, stage-diving even when there was nobody in the audience, regularly risking an injury. Green River's lead guitarist was a guy named Steve Turner, an avid listener of 60s garage-punk, while their rhythm guitarist was Stone Gossard.

Steve and Stone had met at Seattle's Northwest School: Gossard was the metalhead, while Turner was the punk kid. Steve had immediately hoped to get Stone to join Green River. Truth was, Stone *did* have a difficult personality, but Steve was one of the few people who were immune to it: that cutting humor had no effect on him. And more importantly, Stone had a Gibson Les Paul; it was worth seeing past any compatibility issues.

Jeff Ament didn't quite see it that way: him and sarcasm didn't get along. At least, not *that* kind of sarcasm. When Steve had introduced him to Stone it certainly could have gone smoother.

- "Hi, I'm Jeff", he said, extending a hand.
- "Ooh, Jeff-Diction, what a cool name! I've heard you're from Montana. Do you fuck cows?"[9]

It very nearly came to blows.

But Mark was so eager to have Stone in the band he was even willing to submit to an indoctrination in heavy metal, abandoning his punk roots in favor of Alice Cooper. Stone was constantly bugging everyone about Alice Cooper. "Listen to everything except the first two albums", he would always say. So of course, Mark had decided to listen to precisely those two albums, and had ended up falling in love with *Pretties For You*.

Green River's first official gig took place at a house party in Seattle's Central District, on July 1st 1984. The lineup also included drummer Alex 'Vincent' Schumway. Stone was already officially part of the outfit, but he didn't play with them that night, as he didn't feel ready.

Stone still lived with his parents in Capitol Hill, in the heart of the city. His father was an influential lawyer and his mother worked at city council. Their house became Green River's first rehearsal space.

Jeff was the only member of the band with a *real* job so he could pay the rent: he served coffee at Raison d'Être, a cozy restaurant-bar that was a hub for people involved in the music industry. There wasn't a musician in Seattle who hadn't either sat at those tables or waited on them.

To Jeff, that job was just a stepping stone. He had an objective: he was going to make a living from music. A fact

9 Keith Cameron , *Mudhoney: The Sound And The Fury From Seattle*, Voyageur Press, 2014, p.36

worth noting as it wasn't necessarily everyone's ambition. Jeff knew exactly what direction Green River had to take, and that was to sign a deal with a major record label.

Mark didn't agree; he just wanted to play shows, climb up the lighting truss and set fire to himself on stage. He performed for himself, for his friends and for the members of other punk bands who were headbanging in the audience. There was no ambition.

Green River, 1986.
Photo by Charles Peterson

In the meantime, Malfunkshun continued forging their image and identity. Their live shows were like a game of roulette: there was no way of knowing what number Landrew would pull on the audience. He might throw milk and cereal at them, or he might make his way to the bar during one of Kevin's never-ending guitar solos, wearing his leopard-print jacket and a feather boa around his neck, plucking at his wireless, lilac-colored Kramer Duke from the counter (having a wireless bass was a rarity at the time). Some people swore they once saw him in blue crocodile-textured lingerie.

Among the venues Malfunkshun played most was the Grey Door, the artsy hole-in-the-wall in Pioneer Square, though with enough space to allocate a room to growing pot. No proper entry ticket: what small change you had in your pocket would suffice, like an open donation. There wasn't a night that wasn't packed: those in the mosh pit usually risked their lives, swallowed by a swarm of heads, legs and arms, compactly swaying from one side to the other. When hit by the lighting, their hair gel created trippy optical effects, especially if you were high.

Similar scenes could be witnessed at Gorilla Gardens, a newly opened all-ages music club in what had once been a two-screen movie theatre in the International District, also known as Chinatown (the venue's official name was actually Rock Theatre, but it quickly became known as Gorilla Gardens by its regular clientele). It was the only nightclub that had the guts to host heavy metal and punk events at the same time: one was in the so-called "Omni Room" and the other in the "Gorilla Gardens" room.

The intermingling of punks and metalheads generated a softening of relations between the two subcultures. Until then putting the two factions together in the same club without provoking massive brawls had been unthinkable. According to music critics of the time, it is to this coexistence of the two scenes that the birth of grunge can be attributed. In a 1992 Spin magazine article Jonathan Poneman of Sub Pop Records stated "Most of the early bands who would later be associated with the embryonic ‹Seattle sound› were still playing at Gorilla Gardens, an unsavory all-ages club".

Like most venues of the city in those years, Gorilla Gardens was short-lived, but in that brief space of time, between 1984 and 1985, it hosted events that were unprecedented, with headlining acts such as Hüsker Dü, Sonic

Youth and Violent Femmes. Heavyweights that local bands would open for, finally getting a taste of something bigger than their local scene. For example in 1984 local punk band The Fastbacks opened for an emerging outfit from Los Angeles that was the name on everybody's lips: Guns N'Roses, featuring Andy's friend Duff McKagan on bass. Local legends U-Men opened for Sonic Youth, while *Sound Garden* (as Soundgarden erroneously appeared on flyers at the time), opened for Hüsker Dü.

Malfunkshun also opened for Hüsker Dü, but at the Metropolis.

Gorilla Gardens made the headlines at least a few times during its brief run, always for problems relating to disorderly conduct.

On December 7th 1985, during a concert by hardcore punk band Circle Jerks, a surprise inspection by the police put an abrupt end to the show due to what were deemed fire code violations. The crowd did not take it well and a fight broke out, with bottles flying and the cops beating people with clubs. Somebody set fire to a dumpster, and someone else started damaging the cars parked nearby. When they found a pickup truck filled with bricks the punks added those to their anti-cop arsenal too.

It was an epic riot, and it was all over local media the next day. A memorable event in the making of pre-grunge history.

CHAPTER 12

Deep Six

«You got it. It›s slow SLOW and HEAVY and it's THE predominant sound of underground Seattle in '86».

Bruce Pavitt, writing in the April 1986 issue of the Subterranean Pop *fanzine.*

Bands in Seattle in the mid-eighties didn't like being referred to as part of a so-called "musical scene". In Seattle there was no *scene*, rather a signature sound that was distinctive to outfits in the Northwest.

Given the chronic lack of funds, most bands usually didn't record an album; they first recorded a single, and if that went well, an EP. Laying down a whole album required many sessions in the studio, and even more money.

Chris Hanzsek, a twenty-five-year-old disc-jockey from Boston, had set out to rectify this situation. He had a one-way ticket to Seattle and wanted to experience the city's vibrant musical culture first-hand. He was fed up with the pretentious attitude prevalent in Boston, found everywhere from colleges to concerts, where the audience stood with long faces and folded arms, engaged in useless discussions about technique.

In Boston, like New York, the latest trend was New Wave, where bands approached the stage in a more cerebral and calculated way. Nowhere near as chaotic and raw as the Northwest, where bands still listened to Kiss, Aerosmith and The Stooges, and where *nobody* stood still at a show.

Seattle might have been keeping things low-key, but it was having more fun.

Chris Hanzsek's first move was to open a recording studio using funds donated by his girlfriend Tina Casale, a partner both in life and business. The studios were called Reciprocal Recording and were based in Interbay, a neighborhood on the marina, mostly taken up by the railway switches. The train yard was so close that low frequency noises from the trains seeped into the studio. When a band was mic'd up while a train was passing, all the meters would peg at once and they'd have to take a train break[10]. The rate for a recording session was ten dollars an hour: definitely below average.

Green River recorded their first EP at Reciprocal in 1984, called *Come on Down* and released by much-respected New York-based independent label Homestead Records. It contained six tracks of what would later be acknowledged as the first example of grunge music (but it wouldn't be released until 1985).

Chris Hanzsek had caught on to the sound of Seattle, a gritty sound from a gritty port city, and wanted in. Maybe he could make something happen, maybe even make some money.

Jeff Ament and Mark Arm, who weren't just members of Green River but also fervid minds and catalysts within the music community, suggested Chris produce an album that collected the best examples of the city's sound, a compilation-manifesto of Seattle. Hanzsek jumped on the idea and immediately called to arms six of Seattle's most representative bands. He had the talent, he had the studio, the budget was limited but something good could come out of it.

Malfunkshun were among the chosen bands; it would be their first experience in a real studio, and with it came the possibility, for once, of creating something more structured than the homemade demos they recorded on their boombox.

10 *Reciprocal Recording: The Story of a Recording Studio*, Revolution Come And Gone, Northwest Passage, https://bit.ly/2UkTKZm.

Green River were also in the lineup of course, as were popular outfit The Melvins and the ever-present U-Men.

Each of the bands in this select group had its own distinctive characteristics. U-Men for example, whose formula could be summed up in a synthesis of punk, garage and psychedelia, had earned a record deal with the aforementioned Homestead Records, the same label Sonic Youth were signed to.

The U-Men had found local notoriety thanks to a stunt they pulled at the 1985 edition of Bumbershoot Festival, Seattle's main event of the summer. At the beginning of their set the band's drummer, known to collect zippo lighters, poured a copious amount of vodka into a small pond that had formed in front of the stage. At the end of their performance the singer, John Bigley, set fire to a cloth soaked in alcohol and threw it into the puddle. As it hit the surface an enormous ball of fire rose from the pond, accompanied by a surreal hiss due to the explosion-induced airflow. A single, brief, enormous flame. Dozens of families with their kids ran in a panic, while the usual punk crowd, in the unusual context of a day time show, stood by in stunned silence.

The Seattle-Sound compilation would also include the local outfit Skin Yard, whose co-founder and guitar player was a guy of Italian origins named Mike Giancondino, known as 'Jack Endino'. He had embraced that name because nobody, truly nobody, was able to pronounce his actual surname correctly.

Endino had worked at a naval shipyard for a few years, before leaving to form the band, which initially also included co-founder Daniel House, drummer Matt Cameron and vocalist Ben McMillan.

Last but not least, the compilation would also feature Soundgarden, a stunning four-piece band led by the unique voice of stage monster Chris Cornell.

Contrary to expectations, the compilation would not be recorded at Reciprocal. Hanzsek and Casale had been kicked out of the Interbay HQ by the landlord, so Chris had to resort to working as the sound engineer at Seattle's Ironwood Studios. Here he granted himself some studio time between August and September of 1985. It was agreed that each band would record two or three tracks, in separate and distinct studio sessions.

Malfunkshun's contribution to the record consisted in two tunes: *Stars-N-You* and *With yo' heart (Not yo' hands)*, two of many experiments composed in Bainbridge Island years earlier.

Andy showed up to the studio in his full stage regalia: an iridescent jacket, big, colorful sunglasses and a scarf around his neck. He wanted to be Landrew even without an audience.

The original Deep Six record, the first release on C/Z

The band recorded their two tracks in no time, live to tape with no overdubs except for some rhythm guitar. Hearing what they sounded like in a real recording studio for the first time was both exciting and nerve-wracking.

Only one member per band was allowed in the studio during the final mixing and mastering, but Andy and Regan both showed up: they were Malfunkshun, not just *any* band.

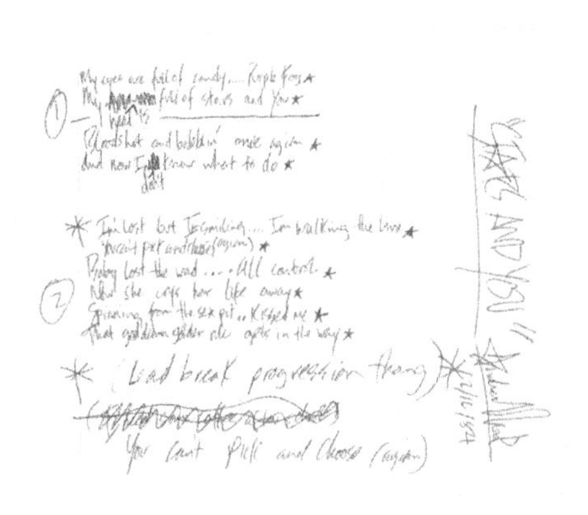

Stars And You handwritten lyrics, by Andy Wood.

The compilation-manifesto of the Seattle sound saw the light of day with the title *Deep Six* and was pressed in two thousand copies. It was the first release of the newly minted label C/Z Records, founded by Chris Hanzsek and Tina Casale. The launch party took place on March 21st and 22nd of 1986 at Union Community Theatre Hall in Seattle Three of the bands involved performed live. Malfunkshun played a track called *My Love,* composed about four years prior.

Deep Six wasn't just punk and it wasn't just metal: it was the undefinable, promiscuous, messy, raw, deafening roar of Seattle's sound.

CHAPTER 13

The old 28-days business

"[Andy] felt so refreshing, just like Monty Python felt to me the first time I saw them. Felt like somebody was opening a door to a whole new way to see the universe that's so much better than the one you remembered the year before you met the person".

- Stone Gossard, interview with the author, 2015

The *Deep Six* compilation represented a turning point for Seattle's musical community, automatically conferring prestige to any band that was part of it. For the first time the city elicited vague interest from the record industry outside of the Pacific Northwest.

In the meantime, Green River, the crown jewel of the compilation, had a problem: they were short one guitar player. Annoyed by the band's transition towards metal, Steve Turner had quit. He was too punk for the affectations, and had started sabotaging their gigs. "He had stopped playing with any kind of distortion, and during at least one show, he had played sitting down on a chair in passive-aggressive protest". [11]

The solution came in the form of Bruce Fairweather, with whom Jeff Ament had gone to college and formed Deranged Diction. Bruce's debut show with Green River took place in the glorious Gorilla Gardens, with Malfunkshun and Soundgarden as the opening acts. It was August 2nd 1985.

---

11 Mark Arm to Mark Yarm for his book *Everybody Loves Our Town: A History Of Grunge*, Crown Archetype, 2011.

The first real moment of truth for Green River came soon thereafter, with their first tour, which, in theory, was to coincide with the release of their EP *Come On Down*. The band did everything themselves, going from one date to the next in Gossard's piece-of-shit station wagon hitched to a U-Haul trailer, used to transport their equipment as well as to sleep in.

Due to bad weather and various bumps on the road, the tour was reduced to a mere seven dates, from Seattle to New York and back. It was rebaptized 'The Prematour', as it had happened too soon, and was plagued by a series of calamities: technical issues, gigs being cancelled at the last minute, fights that broke out because Jeff's hair was too big.

The main problem was the delayed release of *Come On Down*, which ended up not being out by the time they were on the road. This meant Green River were practically unknown outside of the Pacific Northwest.

In hindsight though, it was an epic tour. The fact a band from Seattle was performing outside the state of Washington was a miracle in and of itself, not to mention a chance for Green River to open for some of their idols, like Steve Albini's Big Black or The Minutemen.

Their most memorable performances however took place in Seattle, such as on June 28th 1986 at the Paramount Theatre, opening for P.I.L. (Public Image Limited), the new band formed by John Lydon of the Sex Pistols. The way Mark Arm saw it, Lydon was a former punk idol who had sold his soul to the record industry and therefore deserved to be punished.

"Stick around if you want to see what a real sellout looks like" were Mark Arm's parting words to the crowd before leaving the stage. While P.I.L were performing, their dressing room was being raided by a posse of punks led by Mark Arm and Steve Turner (no longer in the band but present at the show), plus Andy and Regan Hägar, who were also backstage and all wound up. Andy confiscated all the bottles of wine that had been part of Lydon's rider and poured their contents all over the place.

In 1986 Jack Endino, bass player for Skin Yard, contacted Hanszek about a studio that was about to become vacant and proposed a partnership. Reciprocal Recordings reopened in the Fremont neighborhood of Seattle. Green River's second EP *Dry As A Bone* was recorded there, with Endino at the mixing desk as the main producer.

The album was released on newly minted Seattle-based independent label Sub Pop Records, once again with some delay, as Sub Pop found itself broke before it was even out of the starting gate.

But that's a whole different story.

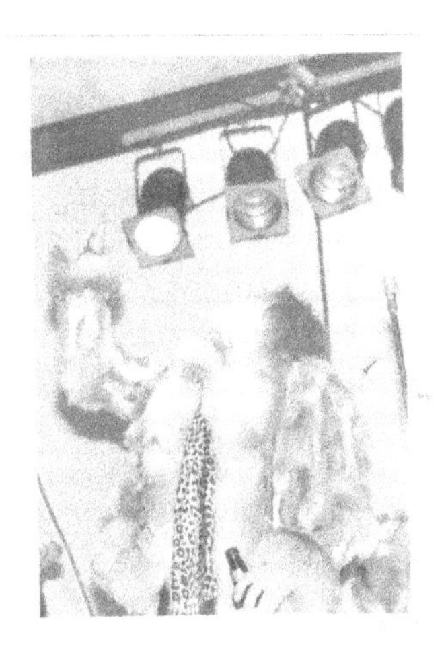

Landrew live, circa 1985. Courtesy of Toni Wood

In the meantime, Andy had outlined his immediate future in his last essay for Bainbridge High: with school over he intended to move to Seattle, where the music was, and finally leave Bainbridge Island behind. Or 'Braindead Island', as he liked to call it.

His chance came soon enough when Blaine Cook, leader of local legends The Fartz and also a good friend of Regan's, went to live in a house owned by his mother, in West Seattle. Blaine needed more housemates with whom to share expenses, in addition to the three already present, so he asked Andy. West Seattle was detached from the rest of the city and kind of a world of its own. Away from the bustle of the city center, which anyway only took fifteen minutes to reach, it was a decidedly cheaper neighborhood to live in. For five wayward punks who were still minors, it was perfect. There was something almost magical about the docks, with their coming and going of cargo ships and rows of colorful containers. Plus, West Seattle had Alki Beach, with its half a mile of beachfront.

The basement of the house Andy moved into immediately became a rehearsal room for Malfunkshun and another local band called The Accüsed. In the kitchen, infested by cockroaches and mice, the walls had been covered with empty boxes of cereal, the main source of nutrition for all the house's residents. Getting enough to eat was always an issue, in spite of the nearby 7-Eleven, stocked with cheap snacks and inexpensive beer, twenty-four hours a day. Luckily there were the girls, often fans, sometimes girlfriends, sometimes just friends. Whatever their official role was, they would frequently to pay for dinner. Some worked in cafés, bars or restaurants and would bring what they could get their hands on: a slice of pizza, a sandwich, a can of Rainier beer.

Food was always welcome because someone always had the munchies; everybody smoked pot. That was on top of whatever else they could get their hands on: acid, cocaine, ecstasy, mushrooms. The recreational use of substances wasn't a secret or a mystery.

Except for Andy. He was using something nobody knew about.

No one had a clue he had crossed the line from recreational use to something more deeply embedded. Not until Kevin started having suspicions.

He had been the one to worry about until then, he was the one with an alcohol problem. His habit had been under control, until he had started to experience blackouts.

One night, he had been more drunk than usual and Toni had reproached him, a bit harsher than usual. It had tipped him over the edge and he had dropped the bomb. A bomb that couldn't be easily diffused.

"You think I'm the one who's fucked up?", Kevin shouted in her face in a blaze of fury. "I'm sorry to disappoint you, but it's your golden boy who's doing needles."

That's how it went with Kevin: he was a dormant volcano that could erupt at any moment.

Toni was speechless.

She had given her boys space to digest the divorce and spend more time with David, and hadn't realized Andy had a problem. And it was a *big* problem, as was evident by the deep track marks she found on his forearms.

Andy was hiding a big flaw in the mechanism that regulated his self-esteem, and heroin was a great way to escape from the grinding of those jammed cogs. Not to mention he was following in the footsteps of his favorite rock stars.

Andy was like a TV game show host[12]: he was always making sure everyone was having a good time. When his problem with heroin surfaced, the cards came tumbling down.

To make matters worse, he had tested positive for Hepatitis B, probably from using a dirty needle. It was at this

12 "Like a game-show host", Chris Cornell interviewed by Katherine Turman, Rip Magazine 10/91, "Life Rules".

point that David stepped in and immediately made Andy check into a hospital. Andy complied, he was too scared of being sick to offer any resistance.

Once that was resolved, Andy started making the rounds of all the nearby rehab facilities, in what he dubbed «the rehab tour». Not exactly the kind of tour he had envisioned when he dreamed of being a musician, but at least he could joke about it. Not that he wasn't scared shitless, but Andy was always good at downplaying problems.

Every single day he and Toni would take the car, Andy at the wheel and Toni in the passenger seat, visiting rehab clinics in Seattle and its immediate surroundings, and every day it would be the same story, as dramatic as it was absurdly comical. Toni would animatedly argue with the medical staff, begging them to take Andy into their care. Andy would mimic the movement of a movie set clapperboard with his arms each time she began another speech to persuade a doctor.

«Aaaaaaand cut! Wow mom, what a dramatic scene!».

Between one clinic and the next they often had lunch at City Picnic, a bar where Andy had briefly worked, and once they even stopped at Best Buy to get a brand new boombox.

Toni put on a brave face, but the truth was she was petrified.

Her son was a junkie. Her golden boy. How could this have happened? Her whole life she had been surrounded by men who were substance abusers, whether alcohol or drugs. When her kids had started experimenting with both she hadn't batted an eyelid. More than that, she had been taught you couldn't trust people who didn't indulge in any vices. *Those* were the dangerous ones.

Of all the clinics they visited, it was Saint Cabrini Medical Centre that finally admitted Andy. On the morning of August 11th 1986 at 8:30 AM Andy was sitting on the steps of the entrance, waiting for Dr. Carlisle, with whom he had an appointment. A few formalities later and the intake procedure was complete, this would be his home for the next twenty-eight days. His file included a picture taken after his first physical. Nothing seems out of place: a lilac-colored Polo shirt, light blue distressed jeans, loose, blond hair, round glasses hanging from his shirt, a proud demeanor, arms folded. The usual Andy.

Andy Wood at The Central, Seattle, 1986, Photo by Charles Peterson

He was now in the care of Dr. Katie Carlisle, a kind lady with delicate manners and a sweet face framed by short, tomboyish hair. Determining her age was tricky, she was probably below forty but the heavy bags under her eyes made her look older.

Dr. Carlisle had herself been a drug addict and now helped those like Andy get clean.

During Andy's stay, she compiled dozens of files on his case, asking him numerous questions. She noticed he often used humor to avoid the more uncomfortable ones. All she would have needed was access to his notebooks and lyrics to know everything about him.

Andy had to keep a diary at the clinic, updating it every day with new entries. He had to write about himself, what had brought him there. And so many forms to fill out, full of questions – the type of questions he had avoided his entire life. One in particular struck him: «What is your experience with wonder and awe?».

An entire album could be written in answer to this question.

CAPITOLO 14

The Sun King

"In his mind, he was already a rock star and he was waiting for the rest of the world to figure it out."

- Chris Cornell, Rolling Stone Magazine, 2016

Andy was discharged from Saint Cabrini Medical Center on September 1st 1986. His certificate of completion of the program reads: "This is your first step towards recovery".

The first.

Malfunkshun were still a band at that point. They were on standby due to Andy's impromptu stay at the clinic but, now that he was out, it was time to move forward, and that meant raising the bar. It had to be admitted, self-management was not yielding the most polished results: none of the band were particularly skilled as sound engineers or PRs. It was probably time to get serious and record some demos worthy of the name. More like how Green River were doing it.

Or like *Soundgarden*.

The backstory on Soundgarden starts on December 12th, 1984, when they make their live debut in a biker bar in Seattle called Top Of The Court, located in an industrial part of town by the Magnolia Bridge. They were not supposed to be on the bill: they fell into place last minute to replace a band named Vexed, which bowed out of their opening slot.

The lineup of the still-nameless trio is Chris Cornell on

drums and vocals, Kim Thayil on guitar, and Hiro Yamamoto on bass. This lineup wouldn't last, though. The band soon realized they needed a full-time frontman, so they enlisted drummer Scott Sundquist (who would be replaced two years later by Matt Cameron), in order to allow Chris to focus on vocals. As the frontman, Cornell certainly fit the bill: he had rock star looks, boundless sensuality and an edgy, powerful voice with an incredible range. Characteristics that truly made him unique in that scene.

Born Christopher John Boyle ('Cornell' was his mother's surname), Chris was from North Seattle and he'd had a turbulent adolescence. At fifteen he had dropped out of high school and though he had no priors himself, he often kept the company of petty crooks and pushers, with whom he'd occasionally form a band and play drums. He had formed The Shemps at seventeen and two years later founded Soundgarden with Yamamoto and Thayil, who both shared his same fascination for 70s punk and metal.

The name *Soundgarden* was inspired by a public art work on the NOAA (National Oceanic and Atmospheric Administration) campus, which lies adjacent to Magnuson Park, on Lake Washington. It is composed of twelve steel organ pipes that produce strange and evocative sounds when channeling the wind.

When Andy came out of rehab it wasn't a good time in the life of Cornell. Chris had just been fired from Ray's Boathouse, a restaurant with a view of Puget Sound that was a staple of Seattle dining, where he worked as an onboard chef. Now unemployed, he spent his days sipping Jack Daniel's and black coffee while sprawled on his sofa, gazing off into the horizon.

Chris was a solitary guy, he was agoraphobic and had a definite tendency to isolate himself. His introspective and analytical nature was reflected in the way he wrote his songs. At the time he was looking for a housemate to split the expenses of his new apartment in Capitol Hill, and he had asked Stone Gossard.

Stone still lived with his folks, also in Capitol Hill, and had no intention of moving out. "But Andy Wood just got out of rehab and is looking for a place to stay", he told Chris.

Andy was planning to go live with his dad on Bainbridge Island, the perfect place to mellow out and slowly get back on his feet. But Chris' phone call changed his mind.

He almost couldn't believe it. To him Chris had always been 'the Sun King'.

The next day Andy had already moved into the apartment on 625 Melrose Avenue, the long street that borders Interstate 5 in its final stretch. Chris definitely had his dark sides, but he was clean; he no longer used drugs. It was essential to Andy's recovery that he didn't share a house with someone who could tempt him to relapse.

None of his friends really had any idea what it meant to go to a rehab clinic, not even Regan. Like everyone else, he didn't understand Andy had a drug *problem*. Regan just thought the situation had gotten a little out of hand and Andy's stint in rehab was more of a stepping stone. He didn't think Andy used any more or less than others, as they were all school dropouts with a lot of time on their hands. Regan had been raised to fear drugs, but then his first experiences hadn't seemed such a big deal, so he had been taking everything and anything under the sun. Unlike Andy, who felt guilty, and was shooting heroin in secret. By himself.

"Just give me your bong; I'll give it back to you when you get out", Regan had told him a few days before he entered the clinic. Andy hadn't replied. He knew there was no going back. Nothing would be the same.

As well as being housemates, Andy and Chris immediately became friends. Though technically their bands were competing, they bonded over their mutual interests and were complementary in their differences.

Their processes for writing songs were almost completely opposite. Andy could knock them out by the dozen in very little time, improvising everything. Usually only one was any good though. In the same timeframe Chris only wrote one song, but it was the right one. Andy composed instinctively, in one solid motion, while Chris was cerebral and would stubbornly fixate on every little detail.

During their life together they had formed a kind of

ritual: every day they each recorded a song on 4-track tape and then gave it to the other to listen to in the evening. Often more the *idea* of a song than an actual song. One of these was called *Island Of Summer*, a vaguely folksy acoustic number the pair recorded together.

In an attempt to get Malfunkshun back up and running Andy recorded dozens and dozens of mixtapes of the band and distributed them around the city. One was called *Andrew Meets Landrew (And All Heaven Breaks Loose)* and contained solo material.

On many evenings at home Chris would observe Andy as he minutely illustrated and filled the tape covers, accurately inscribing dates, instruments involved, places where they had been recorded, credits. Do-it-yourself as a method of survival.

Chris was also the unwilling spectator of another aspect of the Andy Show, a less fun and creative side: his withdrawal symptoms. Chris was right there with him while he was battling his demons, fighting against the monkey on his back, not knowing what to do with those legs, those arms, that body that was suddenly too heavy for him.

Chris was scared *for* Andy, not *of* him. He was not the kind of junkie that was trouble, stealing money to fund his habit.

Andy wasn't that type of guy.

CHAPTER 15

Plan your work, work your plan

«I am sure Xana loved Andy in her own way.
But what was not to love?»

- Toni Wood, interview with the author, 2015

From the early Eighties throughout the Nineties, a glittering world of gentlemen's clubs, adult theaters, and sex shops thrived on Seattle's First Avenue.

Lusty Lady, Fantasy Unlimited, The Champ Arcade were all well-known places to those looking for entertainment in the form of X-rated movies, peep shows and stripteases. The man behind all these activities was Roger Forbes, a porn tycoon who had been dubbed "The X-rated Paul Allen".

At the counter of Fantasy Unlimited in 1987 was a girl named Xana La Fuente. First thing you'd notice about her was her aggressive and insolent beauty. Tall, black hair and eyes, she resembled a young Cher. Andy had a soft spot for Cher.

Regan Hägar had noticed her while Andy was in rehab and had made a mental note to introduce her to him once he was out of the clinic.

And so he did.

"I'll be right back", he announced before storming out, as if Xana could have cared. He ran upstairs, where Andy was harboring the idea of buying a guitar.

"Your future wife is downstairs", he announced, leaving him somewhat perplexed.

Xana's beauty would have intimidated anybody, but Andy confidently strutted right up to her. She was hardly impressed as she squared him up and down, seeing his brown corduroy pants and mismatched clothing. "Lame outfit", she thought.

The good news was Xana's shift was over; someone had just come in to take over for her.

Andy watched as she grabbed her things – a black hat and a guitar. Who knows if it was just for show, or she actually know how to play.

She exited the store, with Andy and Regan following close behind, feeling like two awkward teenagers.

"Are you stalking me?" she eventually asked with annoyance, accompanying the question with an with a gross hand gesture hand gesture.

But Andy had decided he had to at least *talk* to her.

To break the ice he told her about their band, famous throughout Seattle, "Malfunkshun. You ever heard of Malfunkshun?". He took out a poster, one of the most disturbing ones, showing him, Regan and Kevin shirtless, covered in white greasepaint and leaning on a big tombstone.

Xana thought the poster was creepy, but she stopped to chat anyway.

That was Regan's cue to discreetly leave her and Andy alone, after which the pair talked at length before Xana gave Andy her number.

From that moment on they were inseparable. Not a day went by without Andy going to Fantasy Unlimited to see her, where they would talk for an hour or two. Then he would go somewhere else and maybe be back at the end of her shift. Or they would meet at a park, and walk hand in hand for hours, nothing more.

Originally from Santa Fe, New Mexico, Xana had moved to Seattle a year earlier, for love of what was now an ex.

One of her passions was making hats and clothes, she had a great eye for fashion and had dressed many people in the local music scene. And her own appearance was always original and intriguing.

Before she knew it Xana was posting Malfunkshun flyers around the streets of Seattle, and, in short order he had packed her belongings and moved in with Andy and Chris.

Poster for Malfunkshun's gig at the Vogue, February 24th 1986.

During this time Malfunkshun had been true to their intentions and had decided to record their first real demo, and there was only one man who they trusted for the job: Jack Endino, the best sound engineer money could buy.

When Chris Hanzsek had asked Jack to work with him full-time in the studio, Jack had accepted without giving it a second thought. He had instantly envisioned calling on all the most representative bands in Seattle – basically all his friends – to give a sort of continuity to *Deep Six*.

As a musician and an essential part of the Seattle Sound, Endino knew how to perfectly capture a guitar that was raw, undisciplined, and often played badly. A sound that in many cases was the result of some technical trickery: modifying a chord on the electric guitar, lowering it from E Major to D Minor, thus creating a more intense, deep and disturbing sound. Kim Thayil of Soundgarden was one of the first musicians to experiment with this method, following a tip by Buzz Osborne of The Melvins.

Reciprocal Recording, now in a triangle-shaped log house in the Fremont neighborhood, was where Malfunkshun finally recorded their first real demo, giving shape and identity to the dozens of tracks they had taped as amateurs. They were putting together a respectable calling card with which to present themselves to record labels, prospective agents and the media.

Malfunkshun's recording sessions took place between May and August of 1987, with an Otari 8-track recorder and Jack's studio know-how, in sessions of five or six hours, at the cost of twenty-five dollars per hour. Among the songs to come out of those sessions, some complete, others still in raw form, were *Luxury Bed* (*The Rocketship Chair*), *My Only Fan*, *Winter Bites* and *Until the Ocean*.

By his own admission, Andy threw words together, more interested in how they sounded than in their actual meaning. Yet, in spite of the nonsensical lyrics, the chaos of his life off stage seeped through the verses. They reflect a stark contrast between the extravagant entertainer and the fragile outsider. Two sides of Andy, only one of which was clearly visible to those surrounding him.

Jack Endino admired him, and recognized he had an irresistible comedic streak. He had seen Andy perform various times, and couldn't help but laugh – a unique experience in Seattle, going to a concert and laughing.

During Malfunkshun's recording sessions at Reciprocal, Andy was his usual animated self, but also focused and resolute. He trusted Jack, who wasn't just the man at the controls, the pro who was helping them record a decent demo without skipping any meals. Jack was a father figure to the musicians who gravitated towards him, he was someone they could rely on. Countless times he had ended up saving bands stranded on a street corner with loads of equipment and not a shred of wheels in sight.

Malfunkshun were one of them.

On May 23rd 1987 Redd Kross, an institution of California punk, played at Crescent Ballroom in Tacoma, WA., and opening for them were the best bands in Seattle: Green River, Soundgarden and Malfunkshun. The entrance fee was six dollars and fifty cents.

It would be one of the last times Malfunkshun would share the stage with Green River; indeed it would be one of Green River's very last performances. The differences that had emerged during the recording sessions for *Deep Six* had caused an irreparable rift: Mark Arm was against the commercial direction the band was taking, while Jeff Ament and Stone Gossard couldn't wait to take it further.

In parallel, Stone and Andy had developed a musical affinity and would often jam together, just the two of them, in the rehearsal space their bands were sharing. Andy would play fragments of songs he had recorded on tape, Stone would frame them with some guitar riffs and they would both sing on top. One of these sessions resulted in a song called *A Dream Come True*, with Andy on drum machine and vocals, Stone at the guitar.

Ever since Stone had met him three years earlier in Bainbridge Island, he had clocked Andy's ambivalent nature: that ability to make everyone in a room fall in love with him while concealing an inner fragility.

The news was, something was brewing between two of Seattle's most promising bands: the dissident fringe of Malfunkshun was increasingly playing with the dissident faction of Green River.

The truth was, Malfunkshun just weren't making it. It was The Fartz, not them, on the cover of *The Rocket*, the most important magazine devoted to the Seattle Sound.

Day by day, Andy was increasingly realizing that his aspirations were more aligned with those of Jeff Ament and Stone Gossard than with those of his brother Kevin, and even of his best friend Regan. This led to a side project called *Lords of the Wasteland*, a name taken from the lyrics of *God Of Thunder* by Kiss. Lords Of The Wasteland lineup was Jeff Ament, Stone Gossard, Bruce Fairweather, Andy and Regan. Mark Arm, feeling left out, reacted by forming a parody band called *The Wasted Landlords*, which performed only once.

More than an actual band, *Lords of the Wasteland* was neutral ground on which its members could road test their mutual affinity and experiment with things that would have been impossible in their respective groups, namely covers, prevalently of Led Zeppelin and Aerosmith. A temporary band, in which to improvise and really let loose.

On Halloween of 1987, Green River entered their rehearsal space for the last time; not to practice, but to definitively close a chapter. Jeff and Stone told Mark and the others they were quitting the band.

Mark was stone-faced.

The straw that had broken the camel's back had been a recent show in Los Angeles opening for Jane's Addiction during a brief tour of the West Coast. It was supposed to be a crucial gig for Green River, especially given the number of record execs in the audience, but it had been a disaster.

Mark was not in good shape and was struggling to hit his notes. For a few minutes two band members had abandoned the stage. Mark even had to ask the crowd if there was a drummer in the audience, then somehow they had managed to get it together and finish their set.

one of the very few Lords Of The Wasteland gigs, The Vogue, 12/16/1987.

For Jeff it had been one particular detail that had put the final nail in the coffin: while he was in awe of Jane's Addiction and the huge crowd they drew without even an album out, Mark thought they sucked.

Irreconcilable differences.

What a pity however for Green River to break up right when the masters of *Rehab Doll*, their first real album, had landed on the desk of Sub Pop Records.

"By the way, we broke up yesterday", Jeff told Jonathan Poneman and Bruce Pavitt as he handed them the tapes. They didn't take it too well.

The band that was supposed to mark the grand debut of their newly founded record label had just gone bust.

CHAPTER 16

Parting ways

"When people started talking about Seattle, the scene was long gone".

- Greg Gilmore, drummer for The Living, Ten Minute Warning, Mother Love Bone.

On August 9th 1987 Steve Albini's Big Black held their last official concert at Georgetown Steam Plant in Seattle, a decommissioned plant that now lay as a monument to more prosperous times, when Seattle's inexpensive power and practical streetcar system had attracted a flourishing industry.

The show left an indelible mark on Bruce Pavitt, who had yet to conceive Sub Pop Records. He decided then and there that whatever he was going to do next, it had to have the same magic and intensity of that performance.

Pavitt had moved to Seattle four years earlier after attending Evergreen State College in Olympia, where he had DJed at KAOS FM, the campus radio station. He only aired music that was made and distributed independently, convinced that America's smaller cities had just as much to offer as the big metropolises, maybe even more. Bruce was particularly interested in punk music's regional offshoots, and this had led him to start a fanzine called *Subterranean Pop*, dedicated exclusively to independent punk bands who sent him demos from every corner of the U.S.

The first issue of the zine was printed in two hundred cyclostyled and hand-colored copies. Later a stroke of genius had inspired him to add a mixtape to the zine, basically a compilation of all the bands to keep an eye on.

In 1983 Pavitt made the unconventional move to Seattle, attracted by the city's fervidly active underground scene. From there he started writing a column called 'Sub Pop' for local magazine *The Rocket*. In one of these columns he had defined Big Black «bigger than Elvis, louder than Bo Diddley». He had also opened a store called Fallout Records & Skateboards, in Capitol Hill.

In a brief amount of time Pavitt had created a strategic network of activities that made him a central figure of the musical community. He had been noticed, among others, by Jonathan Poneman, who hosted a show at KCMU-90.3 FM, Washington University's college radio (now KEXP 90.3 FM), and who organized shows at the Rainbow Tavern, a popular venue in the U-District. Jonathan invited Pavitt to his radio show, to talk about what he was doing and this whole movement he was promoting. They immediately hit it off.

A few months later Bruce Pavitt was invited by his fellow Chicago native Thayil to see Soundgarden perform at the Rainbow Tavern, on the night managed by Poneman. It was on this night that the two realized they shared a common objective: to concretely develop the budding artistic talents of this new subculture, by providing musicians with the infrastructure necessary to release their music.

To Bruce, creating an actual label with which to publish music and make records was the next logical step from releasing a fanzine-compilation. But that required capital, and he didn't have any. Poneman, on the other hand, had access to some disposable income. His brother had agreed to lend him fifteen thousand dollars in savings bonds so he could start a label, but only after Poneman had presented him with an actual investment plan.

Sub Pop Records' first release was a compilation called *Sub Pop 100* (July 1986) which included, among others, Sonic Youth from New York, Wipers from Portland, and Steve Albini - without Big Black - from Chicago. It was a triumph of *noise rock*. The tracklist also included Seattle's

U-Men. And it was no surprise, considering the huge part they had played in convincing Bruce Pavitt that Seattle was the place to be.

Sub Pop 100 was pressed in five thousand copies, all of which sold-out: a remarkable achievement.

Rehab Doll by the now defunct Green River was the first studio album issued by Sub Pop Records, released in June of 1988. Four months later Soungarden released *Hunted Down/Nothing To Say*, their dissonant first 7" in anticipation of their debut EP *Screaming Life*.

On April 1st 1988, a date that was by no means a coincidence, Sub Pop made its official debut as a business (althought real operations would only start a couple of months later). The label's first "office" was on the eleventh floor of the Terminal Sales Building, an 11-story historical landmark in Seattle's retail core, designed in a terra cotta and brick Gothic-inspired mode in 1923.

Pavitt and Poneman's business strategy was simple. "You offer to put out a local band's record - maybe friends of yours - and you insist that it will be *huge.* But you keep telling the joke. The joke becomes a motto, the motto becomes a t-shirt, the t-shirt becomes a brand, and somewhere along the way, one band's profile explodes into a full-on national hysteria, the brand makes money, and that changes everything».[13] Bruce and Jonathan loved punk. But they also liked Motown.

The winds of change were blowing in Seattle; it was finally on the map of cities that were relevant in music. The goal of playing for fun while holding down a day job was being substituted with the idea of becoming a full-time musician, being able to export the music outside of the city, and signing with a record label.

---

13 Jason Crock, *Bruce Pavitt and Jonathan Poneman*, Pitchfork, July 2008, bit.ly/3rrRz3q, last seen on July 22nd, 2021

Bruce Pavitt (left) and Jonathan Poneman near Sub Pop's first office, at First and Virginia.
Courtesy of Sub Pop Records

Malfunkshun weren't part of this new movement. Not that the word 'break-up' had ever come up. But de facto, once Green River were no longer a band, and given how Lords Of The Wasteland were shaping up, Andy and Regan found themselves practicing increasingly with Jeff Ament, Stone Gossard and Bruce Fairweather and progressively less with Kevin Wood. The sense of unity that had emerged during their rehearsals as Lords Of The Wasteland was further cemented with their first gig at Luna, a shoe store on Broadway, soon to be followed by another gig, at the more hip club The Vogue.

Piqued by the hype that Sub Pop was generating, Malfunkshun had sent in a demo of their recent sessions at Reciprocal.

Both Pavitt and Ponemen liked Andy, and felt that Malfunkshun represented something new and exciting. They invited the band out for lunch to discuss a possible collaboration. One of their conditions was non-negotiable: they wanted Malfunkshun to record an EP, not an album. Condensing their artistic vision into the limited EP format was a dealbreaker for the band, and they declined the offer[14].

Andy didn't give it too much thought, he had other things to think about. He had recently formed the impression that Jeff Ament and Stone Gossard, two of Seattle's top tier musicians, were planning a new band around him.

The idea had actually been Gossard's, since initially Ament had not been on board. His Montana upbringing, forged on rigorous discipline and order, made it hard for him to envision Andy having the necessary control to be the frontman of a determined and ambitious band. "I don't want to have to babysit anybody", he had kept on saying. Then one night he saw Andy play an acoustic set with Stone at Tugs, one of the very first gay bars in Seattle, and he was left speechless. That boy radiated everything Jeff wanted to see in a band.

Maybe he did deserve a chance after all.

A few days later the deal was sealed when Regan and Kevin entered the rehearsal space for the usual Malfunkshun practice session and found Andy playing with Jeff Ament, Stone Gossard and Bruce Fairweather. Plus a new entry: Greg Gilmore, the drummer of Ten Minute Warning, as well as that of one of the most glorious punk bands Seattle had to offer; The Living. They all knew each other in that scene. Gilmore knew who Andy was, and even knew Regan. They would all go to each other's shows, meet at the same record stores, hang out at the same venues, and sometimes even use the same rehearsal space.

In this case though, Regan immediately got the message.

A new path was being forged, and he wasn't part of it.

14 Jonathan Poneman, interview with the author, August 2018

CHAPTER 17

A NEW BAND IN TOWN

"We won't forget Seattle, until we come back and we're all at the Coliseum and we're like, 'Hello Portland! How ya doin!', and everyone boos."

- Andy Wood, *Backlash Magazine interview*, 1988

Though Andy's life was now in Seattle, he would go back to Bainbridge Island almost every weekend. When he was with Xana, they usually went to his dad's: thanks to a hefty veteran pension David could afford considerably more amenities than Toni, including a house she could only dream of.

David was living with a new woman, Gwen, and her son, J.R. It had not taken him long to rebuild his life. (It would not last long though. He would marry and then divorce her shortly after).

What mattered though, was that David treated Xana like a daughter.

Toni was the one who had gotten the short end of the stick with the divorce. She wasn't receiving any alimony and would probably have to work for the rest of her life.

At the time though, it wasn't a big deal. She had a dog and various men buzzing around her. She couldn't say she was unhappy. She *could* say she was free.

When he was alone, Andy preferred to visit Toni. He would wait for her to finish her shift at the retirement home under the big *Town And Country* sign of the local mall. Andy seemed more relaxed without Xana, he didn't have to worry about making sure she was comfortable and having a good time.

Over and over again, there was one thing Andy constantly repeated to his mother. «You know what mom, I'm going to sign a record deal by the time I'm twenty-five».

Twenty-five.

If the road to a record deal meant Malfunkshun had to break up, so be it.

The days of bidding wars between major labels to sign the latest indie band hadn't arrived yet, nor did punk bands aspire to that kind of global success. Punk or not, in his head Andy was a rock star, and only a major record label had the marketing muscle to reach the kind of audience he aspired to.

Toni knew her son's passion for music would take him far. She would observe him as he intently drew his flyers, compiled his demos, prepared his radio interviews.

It wasn't a hobby, Andy was systematically molding his future.

In that period Toni would often think back to a particular episode, when the family was still a unit and were living in Kerpen, Germany. One morning she and Andy, who was three at the time, had gone to the American Consulate in Bonn to settle some paperwork. In the waiting room there were some records and a record player and Toni's gaze had fallen on a *Sesame Street* album. She had taken the record out of its sleeve, placed it on the turntable and put the needle on the groove. When the chorus of *Let's Go Driving* started Andy had been transfixed, utterly intent on listening. Then he had exploded into fits of laughter.

"Let's go driving in an automobile
Let's take a ride in a car
Listen to the horn go beep, beep, beep
As we travel near and far
Beep, be-beep, be-beep"

"Again mommy, play it again!"

How far he had come from that small but telling moment.

Sometimes, when she listened to him talking, Toni had the impression Andy not only had the ambition, but the *urgency* to become someone. Maybe the new band would open doors for him; it was after all with Jeff Ament and Stone Gossard, who both had experience in the music industry.

Andy would often mention Stone, or "Stoney" as he called him. He almost held him in as a high a regard as he did Chris Cornell.

"Stoney is the brains of the band, but I'm the heart", he would often say.

Andy was working as a courier for ABC Legal Services, a law consultancy firm in Seattle. It was a day job like any other, like (almost) every other musician had, and never spoke about, in part because it usually only lasted a season. Prior to this job, his friend and former neighbor in Bainbridge Joe Abrams had found Andy a similar position in a store specialized in making and delivering blueprints. Andy had been fired after just a few weeks. He was way too slow. He would stop to chat with clients for hours, almost entirely forgetting to return to the store.

His performance at ABC didn't fare much better. Andy frequently stopped between deliveries, suddenly inspired by something, jotting things down in his notebook. Many of his songs were born in such a way: from ideas that came out of the blue and were quickly captured on paper. Now he needed to find a name for the new band, and it had to be three syllables.

Or otherwise three words.

Three is a lucky number.

One day a name with no apparent meaning popped into his head during a delivery, so he stopped under a bridge with his hazard lights blinking. It wasn't the most amazing name ever, but it was better than anything the other members of the band had come up with. Stoney had freely quoted Iggy Pop when he pitched the name 'Dum Dum Boys', while Greg Gilmore had offered 'Daddy Long Legs'.

Andy had made it absolutely clear that under no circumstances whatsoever would he ever sing in a band called 'Daddy Long Legs'.

'Mother Love Bone.'
That was the name.
He pitched it to the others.
They liked it.

Apart from the band's name, Andy was perfectly aware of the fact that sooner or later he would have to make a choice.

And he wasn't going to choose Kevin.

He had, though, completely chosen Xana, and they were going to live together, just the two of them. They had rented a two-bedroom apartment in Capitol Hill, not too far from the one they had previously occupied with Chris. In the short time since they had met, Andy and Xana had quickly become each other's sweetest obsession. Both were egocentric artists who loved being at the center of attention, and they fueled each other's creativity. In their new love nest they played music, applied makeup to each other, traded clothes, and spoke for hours about what it might be like to live in another time and place.

Xana would construct magnificent costumes and bizarre hairstyles for Andy.

When the night didn't involve going out, performing

live, or going to see somebody else's gig, Andy would strum his bass, while Xana would sew, or paint stars on jeans, with the music resonating throughout the room.

Xana had no idea what heroin was, nor did she know anybody who had gone to rehab. She was only seventeen.

Andy had told her about his problem with drugs and his stay at the clinic. He had even told her about how his "skin went yellow" from the hepatitis.

Xana had immediately recognized the importance of keeping Andy in check. She realized she would have to protect him from everything that he liked but that was bad for him.

She began asserting herself with small gestures, picking him up from work to make sure he didn't hang out with the wrong crowd, sifting through his lyrics, crossing out any reference to drugs with a red pen.

Andy allowed it.

Xana believed in his talent and wanted him to spend more time developing it, rather than stealing moments between one delivery and another.

"From now on your job will be to stay at home and write songs", she proclaimed one day. "I make enough for both of us".

At the time it was quite common in Seattle (but also elsewhere), for young musicians to be financially supported by young women with stable incomes.

Andy didn't need to be told twice and jumped at the opportunity: he had a band with a bright future ahead of it to put together.

Planning ahead was one of the defining characteristics of Mother Love Bone, something that could definitely not be said for Malfunkshun. Jeff Ament, who had previously handled the management of Green River, knew how to navigate the treacherous seas of contacts and public relations that were necessary to make a splash in the music industry. Music business was certainly less thrilling than music *making*.

Both Jeff and Stone knew the path the band needed to take: straight towards a record deal with a major label. It didn't matter how much the label offered, what mattered was that they got signed. And that whoever they signed with actually cared about the band.

Everybody had a clear vision of what they wanted: Stone wanted composer credits. Greg Gilmore, the only true virtuoso in the band, had strong opinions about how the band should sound, but wasn't interested in the business side of things. His aspiration was to be a full-time musician without having to resort to miserable day jobs. Same for Jeff Ament. Bruce Fairweather only cared about playing his guitar in a rock band and touring the world.

Andy wanted what he had always wanted: to be a rock star.

He had wanted it before any of the others, more than all the others.

Mother Love Bone's very first show took place at the OK Hotel in Seattle on April 22nd 1988. The band played various original tunes, including a song called *Holy Roller*, written months earlier when they were known as Lords Of The Wasteland.

The OK Hotel was a radical art club in a somewhat rundown building, situated under the Alaskan Way Viaduct. More relevantly though, it was one of a handful of venues to have somehow bypassed the dreaded Teen Dance Ordinance that set the age limit to enter clubs at twenty-one, forcing venues to implement a series of security measures.

This was one of the reasons that prompted Mother Love Bone to question whether Seattle was the right place for their rise to stardom. Wouldn't it be better to be in Los Angeles for example, at the pulsing heart of hard rock? L.A. was where Poison and Mötley Crüe were based, it provided fertile ground from which major labels would regularly pick ripe talent.

But first they had to flood labels and management agencies with demos, and that was a job for Jeff. The contacts he had made while in Green River were now worth gold.

Greg Gilmore would anyway never move to Los Angeles permanently. He had been there three years earlier with Duff McKagan, his former band member in Ten Minute Warning, and he had been disappointed. The city was more concerned with music business than with music itself. Duff on the other hand had stayed in L.A., where he played bass in Guns N' Roses.

Kevin Wood also had his eyes on Los Angeles. He still had big plans for Malfunkshun and found it annoying when people commented «What a pity you broke up».

Broke up? Who said the band had broken up?

The fact remained that things were not going as he had anticipated.

Kevin had no intention of joining Mother Love Bone. Also, nobody had asked him to. What Kevin wanted was for Andy to convince Jeff and Stone to join Malfunkshun; Regan and him had discussed the need for a bass player and a rhythm guitarist.

Kevin had given up on college for Malfunkshun and now he was in a deadlock, forced to accept the decisions made by others. It was an unbearable situation for someone who was used to always running the show. He had been the steady and determined leader of the household, a beacon to his brothers, the calm director of events. But this time, for some strange reason, Kevin did something completely uncharacteristic. He passively let events unfold.

One thing was clear; he needed a new band.

CHAPTER 18

My Anger Is Joy

"Andy had such a big- arena-rock-show presence. Even a little club like The Vogue which seemed like it could barely hold a hundred people, he treated the crowd like it was a hundred thousand."

-Damon Stewart, KISW DJ, Sony Music regional A&R scout (quote from *Everybody Loves Our Town*, by Mark Yarm)

Aberdeen, WA, is a dull and rather anonymous town about two hours by car from Seattle. It's primarily known for its lumber industry, so much so it was baptized "the lumber capital of the world". It was also known for another defining characteristic: monotony.

One afternoon in January of 1988, Jack Endino received a phone in his Reciprocal Studios from the Aberdeen area code. On the other end of the receiver, a mild voice told Jack he was calling on behalf of Dale Crover, drummer for The Melvins. He and his band wanted to record a demo at Reciprocal Recordings.

The Melvins were considered royalty in Seattle: if Crover played with this kid, there must be something there, thought Endino, so he agreed.

A few days later, the kid on the phone arrived at Reciprocal along with Crover and a very tall bassist. The kid had the same gloomy demeanor as his city, pale skin, stubble on his chin, long, blond hair and light, almost transparent blue eyes with a lively light flickering in them. There was a certain harmony to his disheveled appearance.

All in all, he was a handsome guy.

On January 23, 1988, the nameless band, whose lineup included, besides the pale guy, local bassist Krist Novoselic, with Dale Crover of The Melvins sitting in on drums and backing vocals, recorded and mixed ten tracks in five hours. The last song they were recording, titled *Pen Cap Chew*, risked spilling into overtime. The multitrack master tape ran out just at the start of the second chorus, and the band didn't want to buy another reel, so Jack just faded it out, and called it a day.

Endino didn't really know what to make of what he was hearing, but the singer, the blond kid who had made the phone call, had an excellent melodic approach and a very incisive voice. It was a powerful roar, and Jack had not heard many singers that could compare.

At the end of the session Endino asked if he could keep a copy of the demo. He wanted to get it heard, specifically by Jonathan Poneman.

Since the band didn't have a name yet, he just wrote "Kurdt's band" on the cassette.

A month later, in that same studio, it was time for the newly formed Mother Love Bone to record their first demo. It was February 19th 1988, and the band had planned to record five songs in four sessions.

Greg Gilmore was the first to arrive in the studio to set up his drum kit, it took him hours to get it just right. The rest of the band arrived later in the afternoon, positioned the amps and then did a soundcheck. Before recording they took a quick break at the gas station, with JoJos[15] and beer for all. When the band returned to the studio, Jack was no longer at the mixing desk; he was in the booth, playing Greg's drums. To make matters worse, he had moved all the mics.

«I thought it would take you longer!».

15 Extremely greasy, deep fried figer-sized potato wedges. Known by this name in the Pacific Northwest.

That was typical of Jack: not to waste a second of a band's downtime by recording *something else*.

Despite the fact they hadn't rehearsed much, once Mother Love Bone started recording, they sounded like they had been playing together for years. Stone and Jeff were the ringleaders, but without overshadowing anyone else, least of all Andy.

What was taking shape in those studios reflected the general tendency of Seattle's scene at the time: to make songs that were intended to be hits, to be radio-friendly, to be embraced by a wider audience. It was a kind of contemporary hard rock that emulated one of the novelty acts of the moment ⊠ Guns N' Roses ⊠ but was firmly rooted in the classics, like Led Zeppelin, Black Sabbath, Kiss.

The first two recording sessions flew by. Only a few songs were finished and arranged; others, like *Half-Ass Monkey Boy*, with its heavy riff, were more loose improvisations and would have to be rerecorded at a later date, once they had been given more structure.

The final mix included ten tracks: *Showdown, Holy Roller, Jumping Jehovah, Lubricated Muscle Drive, Capricorn Sister, One Time Fire* [16]*, Stargazer, The Other Slide, Lady Godiva Blues and Zanzibar.*

In the first days of April 1988, not long after the official inauguration of Sub Pop Records, the band of the pale-faced kid called Kurdt played its first official concert at Seattle's Central Tavern, one of the oldest-running taverns in the city. Endino had given their demo to Poneman, who had found it interesting. In particular, Poneman's jaw had dropped upon hearing the opening track, *If You Must*, with its primordial scream in the hook. He had listened to it over and over again.

Up to that point the band had gone by the names "Ted Ed Fred" or "Pen Cap Chew", depending on Kurdt's mood,

16 *One Time Fire* got re-worked by Stone Gossard after Andy's passing. It evolved into *E'Ballad*, included in the so-called *Gossman Project*, and eventually turned into Pearl Jam's massive hit *Black*.

and had played prevalently at friends' house parties, or in small church theatre halls in Olympia or Tacoma.

In addition to Kurdt, the lineup included bassist Krist Novoselic and a new drummer, Dave Foster. At their show at the Central, excluding the band itself, Poneman, Pavitt, various girlfriends and the bar staff, the venue was empty. Deciding there was no point in playing an entire set, they only performed one song in its entirety, *Love Buzz*[17], which was a cover to boot. On April 24th 1988 the band, with the same lineup, performed at The Vogue, opening for Blood Circus and Fluid, both signed to Sub Pop.

The real news however, was that Kurt's band was looking for a new rhythm guitarist, and they had their eyes on Kevin Wood. His raw guitar playing was exactly what the band needed.

In the meantime Malfunkshun were in a transitional stage. They hadn't actually broken up yet, but were kind of in stand-by mode. To squash the gossip surrounding the band's demise, Andy had written a statement for *Backlash Magazine*.

> "In an attempt to dispell rumors contrary to fact, Landrew, Kevin and Regan, members of Seattle's loverock power trio, wish to announce they are still together..."

Nevertheless, there was tension and an air of uncertainty. Kevin and Regan found it difficult to imagine a future for *Mfunk* with Andy launching another musical endeavor.

In any case, Andy wasn't the only one who had to justify his choices. Stone Gossard also felt the need to explain to Regan why he had been excluded from Mother Love Bone. A rather rare event, as Stone wasn't the type to account to others.

The two of them had spent so much time together, teas-

17 John D. Luerssen; *Nirvana FAQ: All That's Left to Know About the Most Important Band of the 1990s*, Hal Leonard Corporation, March 1st 2014

ing their hair into voluminous coifs, improvising songs and downing keggers. But this wasn't about friendship.

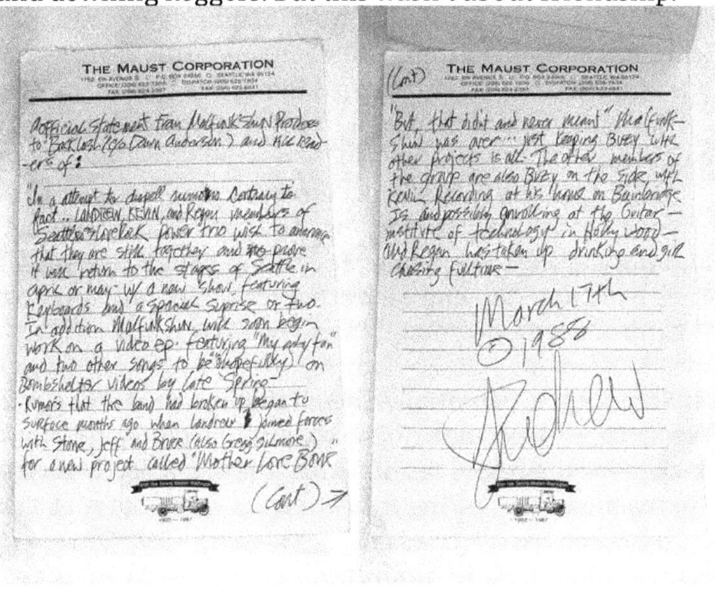

THE MAUST CORPORATION

Official Statement from Malfunkshun Productions to Backlash (c/o Dawn Anderson) and the readers of:

"In a attempt to dispel rumors contrary to fact.. Landrew, Kevin, and Regan members of Seattle's Lovelek power trio wish to announce that they are still together and we prove it with return to the stages of Seattle in april or may w/ a new show featuring keyboards and a special suprise or two. In addition Malfunkshun will soon begin work on a video ep. featuring "My only fan" and two other songs to be (hopefully) on Bombshelter videos by late Spring-

Rumors that the band had broken up began to surface months ago when Landrew joined forces with Stone, Jeff and Bruce (also Gregg Gilmore)" for a new project called "Mother Love Bone

(Cont) →

(Cont) THE MAUST CORPORATION

"But, that didn't and never meant" Malfunkshun was over.. just keeping busy with other projects is all. The other members of the group are also busy on the side, with Kevin recording at his house on Bainbridge Is. and possibly enrolling at the Guitar Institute of Technology in Hollywood — and Regan has taken up drinking and girl chasing full time —

March 17th
© 1988
Andrew

Andy Wood's handwritten press release, addressed to Backlash Magazine's Dawn Anderson, March 17th, 1988

"Gilmore's in the band now. Don't take it personal", Stone had told Regan on the phone. Gilmore was simply the best drummer on the market; the only guy who could compete was probably Matt Cameron.

But he played in another band.

On May 6th 1988, Malfunkshun performed at the Community World Theater in Tacoma, opening for Skin Yard, Jack Endino's band. It turned out to be a pivotal gig for a number of reasons.

Firstly, it was where a local drummer called Chad Channing was introduced to Kurt and Krist for the first time by a common friend. He would end up joining Kurt's band shortly thereafter, replacing their former drummer Dave Foster.

Chad, a twenty-year-old from Bainbridge Island, had learned to play the drums while rehabilitating from a serious accident that had broken his femur. He had bushy eyebrows and a face that looked like it was drawn by a crazy cartoonist.

Chad was a big Malfunkshun fan, plus he was good friends with Kevin as they used to ride bikes together, and work at the same fish restaurant in Bainbridge Island. They had been knowing each other for some time, after being introduced by common friend Rob Day.

Secondly, a potentially life-changing event for Kevin Wood took place that night; something he would think back to for the rest of his life. After the gig, Krist Novoselic approached him, asking if he'd like to hang out and jam with the band sometimes.

Kevin had no doubt in his mind: they were old school punk, a phase he had outgrown ages ago. He wasn't interested, and declined.

Kurt's band would pick a name after Chad joined. They would be called 'Nirvana'.

That gig in Tacoma would end up being Malfunkshun's last.

Another detail Kevin had not foreseen, at the time.

PART 3

CHAPTER 19

Dreaming big

"It's good to be back, but I'll tell you quite frankly, I feel like fucking shit. We took a plane early this morning, and Scottie Olsen our man at the soundboard said: 'Take some of these and you'll be alright'. I took a couple of them, and this morning in the hotel room my fucking ESPN turned into the Disney Channel!"

- Andy Wood, Seattle's Central Tavern, December 10th, 1988

Denny Swofford was a eighteen-year-old kid from Portland, Oregon, who had moved to Seattle in March of 1988: he knew something big was happening in the scene, but he hadn't realized the true scope of it until he saw Mother Love Bone perform at the Moore, a Seattle landmark and one of the longest-running theatres in the city. He spent the entire evening by the mixing console, transfixed by that charismatic figure on stage, with his feather boa, long black gloves, and a theatricality reminiscent of Freddie Mercury. Denny had never heard of the band before, quickly felt the urge to record the entire show, while a friend of his took some photos.

At the end of the set Andy got down from the stage and walked past the mixer, where he was promptly stopped by Denny, who told him he had recorded the entire gig. Andy was thrilled. Not the typical "why are you recording my stuff?" kind of attitude. He was anxious to *hear* his band live.

Denny had done it once; he could do it hundreds of times more. It could even turn into a job.

All Denny knew was that he was entranced by the band, and he needed to be where they were.
Wherever that was.

In an interview for the August-September 1988 issue of *Backlash Magazine*, Andy, Greg, Bruce, Stone and Jeff tried to explain what distinguished Mother Love Bone from their previous bands. Purist fans of Green River and Malfunkshun were not happy about the fusion of the two outfits: too much ambition, too much drive to succeed. So much so that the interview was published with the title «Mother *Lovebone* [sic] sell their souls».

To be fair, one of the many reasons Green River ended up disbanding, was that Jeff and Stone had a terrible habit of inviting record execs to their shows, while Mark wanted to only put friends on the guestlist. Most of the time the record execs never even showed up, except for Anna Statman, at the time part of Slash Records, later A&R of Geffen Records in its L.A. headquarter.

Even though Mother Love Bone had decided against moving to L.A., it was nonetheless a territory they looked towards and combed through for useful contacts, something that Jeff had done exceptionally well. One of the many MLB demos he had circulated, had landed on Statman's desk at Geffen. Since then she had started calling him every day, leaving dozens of messages on his answering machine, exhorting him to set up a meeting as soon as possible. Most of all, she wanted to see the band live.

Jeff would never have let such an opportunity slip through his fingers. His band wasn't like Soundgarden, who had preferred to publish their debut album *Ultramega OK* on independent label SST, rather than put themselves in the hands of a major record label. It was a decision that reflected Soundgarden's loyalty to their own roots.

On September 24th 1988, Mother Love Bone performed at the Paramount Theatre. It was one of those nights in which the audience wasn't enough to even cover the expenses of opening the venue. A couple of month later, on December 10th, they performed at the Central Tavern, for the one-year anniversary party of *Backlash Magazine*. The band were remarkably tight considering their relatively limited experience performing together, and did a ten-track set that opened with *Through Fade Away*. By then Andy had abandoned the outrageous makeup he had adopted with Malfunkshun, but he was still in the habit of dressing garishly and directly addressing the audience, telling anecdotes between songs and establishing direct contact with the fans in the first rows, particularly the female ones.

"Hey if the girl down here doesn't stop grabbing my balls, she's outta here".

In this phase the band often played at The Vogue, which was known, among other things, for the colorful assortment of drag queens that worked behind the bar.

The Vogue had risen from the ashes of Wrex, a historical gay bar for bikers in the eighties, and had become a mecca for those who wanted to be seen.

It smelled faintly of vanilla, the result of all the poppers that were being consumed.

The promoters who organized events at The Vogue poured blood, sweat and tears (not to mention money) into each event, and the long-lasting friendships that were often forged between the venue's personnel and members of the audience made it all worth it.

Once a week the room in the back would be monopolized by the DJs of radio KISW 99.9FM. Among them was DJ personality Mike Jones, surrounded by a swarm of musicians and promoters, all enveloped in a thick cloud of smoke.

It was during a gig at The Vogue, on July 4th 1988, that the future of Mother Love Bone was to take shape. That night would mark their first step into the world of major label music business.

Nobody had any doubts that MLB were about to blow up and would soon be at the center of a bitter feud between labels.

Nobody believed this more than Xana.

Ever since she had been welcomed into the Wood family, everyone had realized how valuable her presence was to Andy. She was doing everything in her power to keep him clean.

She followed him everywhere, participated in his decisions, created his stage looks, and was an integral part of the band's entourage.

Andy was thrilled to have Xana around all the time: he felt protected.

He liked it when other people decided for him, especially women. Plus, Xana surely wasn't like Denise, who had welcomed him back from rehab by passing him a bong full of cocaine.

The fact remained that it was certainly no simple task to stay clean outside of the clinic. The streets of downtown Seattle were littered with all the substances Andy was supposed to steer clear of.

As for Toni, she was perplexed. She knew Xana loved her son, but she would have preferred it if Andy had waited a little longer instead of jumping into a serious relationship straight out of rehab.

Andy's bond with the opposite sex had always worried her. He was too vulnerable, too easy to manipulate. His relationships always turned into turbulent and problematic ordeals.

The same was true of Kevin and Brian: there was always a point of no return in which love became open warfare, a question of life or death. Brian had always believed that "the true value of a relationship between a man and a woman is friendship, but then love comes along and ruins everything".[18]

---

18 Scot Barbour, *Malfunkshun, the Andrew Wood Story*, Universal /The Maze, 2005

Andy was completely smitten. He was head over heels for Xana, his life revolved around her.

The feeling was mutual, the relationship was passionate and enthralling.

The prospect of the band signing a contract with Geffen electrified Xana as much as it did Andy.

She didn't mind financially supporting him as he pursued his dream of becoming a rock star. On the other hand, that's what many girls did for their wannabe-rockstar boyfriends.

Then again, becoming rich didn't sound too bad either.

CHAPTER 20

Another bottle of Beaujolais

"Andy was a rock star even if there were only six people there. He would talk to the balcony even if there wasn't a balcony in the club."

- Michael Goldstone, Rolling Stone, February 6, 1997

Ken Alan Deans and Kelly Mark Curtis were both born and raised in Seattle.

They had met when Deans was still the drummer in a band called The Heats, and Curtis was working as Heart's publicist. The Heats and Heart had been on tour together, and in that time Deans and Curtis had become friends.

In 1986, after both had worked separately in band management, they relocated to Seattle almost simultaneously and started their own company, Mark Alan Productions. Since they had suffered significant financial losses in their previous efforts, they had resolved never to manage bands again. Instead the new company focused on production for the increasing number of promoters that were coming through with national tours: Portland, Seattle, Spokane and Vancouver were their areas of interest.

Mark Alan's office was right across the street from the Grand Central Bakery, on First Avenue South, where Stone Gossard worked as a busboy. One day Deans was having lunch there, and immediately recognized Stone as the former guitarist of Green River. Stone also recognized Deans, and took advantage of the opportunity to hand him a Mother Love Bone demo the band had recorded in February/March 1988 at Reciprocal.

When Deans played it back in the meeting room of his

and Curtis' office, he thought the band had potential. Curtis, on the other hand, was not particularly impressed. They sounded pretty bad, he thought.

Some time later, Curtis received a phone call from Anna Statman at Geffen Records, asking him to accompany her to see Mother Love Bone perform at the Vogue. The performance took place on July 4th 1988 and it was an eye-opener for Kelly, a game changer for the band and the beginning of an inexorable ascent.

Curtis had been convinced by their performance, but not by their demo, so he asked Statman if she could finance a brand new one, to be recorded with a producer of Geffen's choosing, and to be exclusively at the disposal of the label. The cost of this operation was five thousand dollars and in exchange, Geffen wanted Mark Alan Productions to manage the band.

The demo, produced by Bruce Calder, was recorded in just a couple of days at Lawson Studios in Seattle (later Bad Animals Studios), after which both the band and Kelly flew to the Geffen offices in Los Angeles to meet with its president, Eddie Rosenblatt. It became immediately clear that something big was going to happen.

Mark Alan Productions *would* be involved in band management again after all, but Mother Love Bone would not be the only band they would take under their wing.

Having picked up on the hype that was building around Mark Alan Productions and their new protegées, ASCAP[19] started sending them label representatives and affiliates. One day a local promoter called Randy Hauser stormed into their office. "Hey, I've got this band called Diamond Lie. I think they're pretty good. Would you check them out and consider joining me in managing them?»

Hauser was a hairdresser by day and a small-time pusher/events promoter by night, a veteran of the Seattle music scene from well before it could be called a scene. He'd had some issues in the past with cocaine and had even

19 American Society of Composers, Authors and Publishers.

been arrested on drug charges, but he was well-connected to many A&Rs and Deans trusted him.

So they all went to the Music Bank, a unique and epic music hostel under the Ballard Bridge where musicians could rent a room and rehearse 24/7; to say it with the words of Ken Deans himself, "if there was ever a version of Seattle's Chelsea Hotel, the Music Bank was *that* place". [20]

It was basically a big warehouse sectioned off with plywood walls and it probably didn't meet all the fire code regulations, but it was cheap. The members of Diamond Lie - all four of them - lived there.

As Deans and Curtis walked through the door of the Music Bank, they were met with a cacophony of sounds. The floor was littered with a dozen half-empty cases of Rainier Beer. The band, consisting of singer-songwriter Layne Staley, guitarist Jerry Cantrell, bass player Mike Starr and drummer Sean Kinney, were living in a 20ftx20ft unit, the size of a small garage. All of them were sleeping on the floor. It must have been two in the afternoon, apparently still a little too early for them.

It didn't take long for Deans and Curtis to realize that half of the warehouse was being used to grow cannabis.

So, basically, the Music Bank was home to two distinct operations: the front, with the rental of cheap rooms to rehearse in, and the back, the pot growing operation, which eventually got busted.

The Music Bank was a melting pot of creativity, a hub for musicians, with all these bands coming together in one place where they could just jam and hang out. Every night would turn into an impromptu party going back and forth between the rooms, almost a club-like atmosphere.

Staley and Cantrell would have been homeless had it not been for the Music Bank. Likewise, Kinney and Starr also had no stable place to live. Backstage at a gig one night, Diamond Lie decided to switch its name to Alice In Chains.

20 Ken Deans, interview with the author, February 2019.

In the meantime Deans had booked them a slot at London Bridge Studios to record a demo[21].

As things progressed with Alice In Chains, Deans and Curtis found themselves clashing on how to manage the band. Deans aimed to preserve their group chemistry, while Kelly just did not want to deal with addiction-related issues that existed within the band. For a while, so it seemed, he had even planned to pull Cantrell out of Alice In Chains and focus on him as a solo artist, or build a new band around him.

DIDA: ticket for Summer Rock '88, Skate King, Kent, September 1988

Having spent a lot of time with the guys in the studio, Deans knew this would not be an option. So, his solution was to call in Susan Silver, a prominent figure in the Seattle music environment who had managed bands like the U-Men and The Screaming Trees, and was, by that time,

21 Soon to be known as *The Treehouse Tapes*.

managing Soundgarden (incidentally, she was also Chris Cornell's soon-to-be wife).

Hoping to safeguard the band's integrity, Deans gave Silver space in his office, plus his share of Alice In Chains. So, in the end, Silver was in charge of managing AIC along-side Curtis, who would also be in charge for Mother Love Bone.

From that moment on, the two bands would frequently share the same stage. First time it was on August 11th 1988 at *Summer Rock 88*, a festival that took place at Kent Skate King, a roller rink south of Seattle. At the time it was com-mon for concerts to be organized at roller rinks.

That night, pulling who knows what strings, Randy Hauser had managed to get some people from Capitol Records to come check out the performances. "Seriously, you got us out here to see some loud, mohawk-wearing punks?", had been one of the comments.

While AIC were performing, Staley had seen Andy and Bruce in the crowd and had called out to them to join him on stage to perform a cover of David Bowie's *Suffragette City*. But Andy had grabbed Bruce's arm and dragged him away, pretending not to hear. Before Alice In Chains were the slick heavy metal band the world would come to know, they were viewed as a cheesy glam band, and not the kind of outfit Andy or Mother Love Bone aspired to associate themselves with.

For both bands, Kelly Curtis was more than just a man-ager. He was a father figure who was strongly protective of his musicians, often providing accommodation at his house when they needed a place to stay, as was the case with Jerry Cantrell after he left the Music Bank.

As things stood, Geffen Records had been the first ma-jor label to come forward for Mother Love Bone. But as promising as things had seemed when they had started, negotiations were at a standstill. The band was becoming increasingly dubious about Geffen being the right choice for them, and this assessment was cemented by their impression of Tom Zutaut, a man who usually came into play only when the stakes were really high. Zutaut was the guy who had signed Guns N' Roses, the most promising band in L.A., and had been hired by Anna Statman to reel MLB in after she had noticed the band's progressive loss of interest in Geffen.

The first time the band met Zutaut was in the lobby of the Four Seasons after a show at the Central Tavern. Zutaut arrived forty-five minutes late. Kelly Curtis invited him to sit at the bar, but Zutaut stood still where he was. Anna Statman also remained as she was: sitting on the floor in a corner. An image that perfectly captures the dynamics at play, because from that moment on, Statman would no longer have a say in proceedings.

Both the band and Kelly Curtis were increasingly put off by Zutaut. He wasn't transparent, he didn't make any concrete offers, and he made snide comments on the alleged drug use of this or the other musician.

From his point of view, Zutaut was almost offended by the lack of enthusiasm the band displayed, as if they hadn't realized the immense privilege of dealing with him.

Kelly and the boys had thus decided to take other offers into consideration. Geffen would no longer be the only suitor vying for their attention. Atlantic Records and its charismatic A&R Jason Flom were also now in the running.

Flom adopted a different approach to Zutaut: he took the band out for expensive dinners, where he would go on lengthy digressions on *Scarface*, his favorite movie, washed down with numerous bottles of Beaujolais.

But this also didn't work.

At this point Mother Love Bone were at the center of a bidding war between major labels and Ament's phone would ring incessantly. Being treated to lavish dinners by record labels became a frequent occurrence.

Andy dubbed it the "restaurant-tour".

Mother Love Bone's next three gigs, two at the Central and one at the offbeat Skate King in Kent, looked more like conventions for A&R reps and music industry insiders than actual shows. It was impossible to move around at any of the three performances without running into the national director, senior vice president, or assistant head schmooze of one record company or another. This included a memorable KISW-FM "Rising Star" show, on November 17th 1988, with Mother Love Bone and Soundgarden opening for Jane's Addiction.

The bitter dispute to sign the band was finally settled in favor of one man: Michael Goldstone, the top A&R of PolyGram Records. It was him, more than the label he represented, that won everybody over.

Kelly Curtis had no doubts: Goldstone was the right person to entrust Mother Love Bone to. He was a visionary, perhaps even a madman, but with his feet firmly planted on the ground. Most of all, he made a solid offer: a deal for seven albums and two hundred and fifty thousand dollars upfront, in cash, to make the first one. Those kinds of sums for a single album were unheard of in Seattle at the time.

Everyone was present at the dinner to seal the deal and sign the contract.

Everyone, except Andy.

CHAPTER 21

THE INSTIGATOR OF THE ME GENERATION

"As we got signed we became serious in terms of the business side, the band became more serious at scrutinizing everything. That stifled our growing process, that stifled our friendships, our ability to know that the reason why we had got to where we had got was because we were irreverent, and we were open to each other. And then we became less open to each other, I think, and more rigid".

-Stone Gossard, interview with the author, 2015

"Mom, what kinda car do you want?"
"What do you mean honey?"
"It said: what car do you want?"
"A Volkswagen Station Wagon"
"I knew it".

It wasn't often that Toni got a call from Andy at work, on the second floor of the retirement home in Bainbridge Island, in the dementia unit.

That day however, Andy was too excited to wait for her shift to end.

«Mom, we signed a record deal: I can buy you all the cars you want!».

Toni couldn't believe her ears; nobody could believe it. Even the band almost couldn't believe it. No one could have imagined a major record label like PolyGram would invest that kind of money in a fledgling outfit with only fourteen shows under their belt and an album still to be made.

That being said, neither the band, nor Kelly Curtis were so naïve as to think that two hundred and fifty thousand dollars didn't come with strings attached. It was the initial budget the label had allocated to finance the first album, and a form of encouragement to the band members. But that first album then had to sell: that money was simply an advance that had to be paid back in record sales. In legal terms, a "recoupable advance".

This was a time when signing a record deal often meant an artist would give up as much as 50% of their publishing rights domestically, and anywhere up to 80% outside the USA and Canada. Signing a contract with a label basically meant a band had to start shopping for revenue streams, such as sponsorships or merch deals. That's where artists got their advance money, because it could take up to eighteen months before they got a royalty account out of the record company. This was a very specific issue many bands didn't take into consideration when signing a contract, and the reason so many found themselves broke even after selling a lot of records.

Alice In Chains took six months to sign their deal with Columbia. Their lawyers wanted to make sure the contract was airtight and the band owned the rights to every inch of their music.

Mother Love Bone's deal with PolyGram was not as fortunate. To tell it straight, for a number of reasons it would turn out to be a very bad contract.

Neverhteless, Andy had other things on his mind; legal matters and paperwork bored him, and he had no desire to spend any time on them. Those were for Jeff, Stone and Kelly to iron out. Andy's role was that of rock star, and following whatever decisions were made by the others. He just wanted to go on tour and hopefully perform in a stadium. "I don't know if somebody is as anxious as me to get into that arena", he stated in an interview for the video-profile PolyGram made of the band. "I want to get on an arena tour with some bands – who cares – Warrant, for that matter."[22]

22 Most of this footage only saw the light in 1993, when it was fea-

In the course of that interview Andy scaled back his enthusiasm about the record deal; sure, it was for seven albums, but it could be renegotiated at any moment. The contract established a monthly pay of six hundred dollars for each band member, the rest of the money would be used to produce the first full-length.

Exhilarated at the prospect of spending their lives on the road, all the members of MLB quit their day jobs except for Greg Gilmore, who continued working in an electronics store, where he would repair appliances, in particular VHS recorders. Never leave a job, unless somebody else is paying your rent: that was what Greg believed.

Michael Goldstone's first move as manager of the band confirmed the good impression he had made on the boys. Following their wishes, he insisted PolyGram allow them to record an EP, not an entire album, as the label was expecting.

In January 1989, Mother Love Bone did a five- days recording session at Seattle's London Bridge Studios. Behind the mixing desk was British producer Mark Dearnley, known for his work with AC/DC (most notably on the album *For Those About To Rock*).

Those five days were enough to give a whole new sound to a handful of songs written at various points in time. Some went as far back as Bainbridge Island, when Andy and Stone would meet up before Green River had even broken up. Others dated back to when Andy was living at Stanley Apartments, a cheap residential building in the neighborhood of First Hill. Stone would visit him and they would record music on their boom box.

---

tured in *The Love Bone Earth Affair*, a mini-documentary including never-seen-before videos of Mother Love Bone live in concert, combined with previously unreleased interviews with the band. The documentary covers the band's formation and its eventual disbandment due to Wood's death. Additionally, the videos for *Stardog Champion and Holy Roller* are included. *The Love Bone Earth Affair* was first released on VHS, with an official DVD version released on November 4th 2016 as part of the boxed set *Mother Love Bone: On Earth as it is - The Complete Works.*

Andy Wood and Stone Gossard, Seattle's Central Tavern, 1988. Photo by Lance Mercer. In the audience: Shawn Smith (1965-2019)

Andy had figured out how to do overdubs using a primitive multi-tracking technique: he'd record a guitar riff on tape, then played it back and recorded himself singing on top. He would play something for Stone, who would then add some guitar licks and lay them down for Andy to sing over. It was in that process that the two of them wrote a song called *Stargazer*, which, inexplicably, didn't end up in the EP.

The tunes which made it into the EP instead were *Thru' Fade Away*, *Mindshaker Meltdown*, *Half Ass Monkey Boy*, and the sultry ballad *Crown Of Thorns*, probably the song that best exemplifies Andy's ability to compose music, as well as his vocal maturity. The lyrics speak volumes, if one reads between the lines: his reference to "Mr. Faded Glory" tells of a relationship falling apart, due to certain bad habits one can't kick. Long story cut short, those lyrics reveal all the torment that regularly pushed Andy to call on the Mexican dealers in Lower Queen Anne.

The closing song of the EP, *Capricorn Sister*, has a ghost track at the end titled *Zanzibar* (an homage to Freddie Mercury), recorded at Reciprocal with Jack Endino a few months prior.

The EP was called *Shine*. Recording it felt a bit like cleaning house to Andy[23].

Mother Love Bone first Polygram promotional poster

23 Andy Wood, *interview with Phil Alexander*, angelfire.com/wa/olympus/articles.html, checked on November 1st, 2016.

Shine was released on March 20th 1989 on Stardog Records, a sub-label PolyGram created to minimize the... major label effect. That was a smart move once again piloted by Goldstone; knowing how worried the band were of losing their street credibility, he had convinced PolyGram to follow the example set by Guns N' Roses, who three years earlier had released their first EP *Live ?!*@ Like a Suicide* on an independent sub-label Geffen Records had created for the occasion, called Uzi Suicide. It was a strategic move intended to retain the band's image as an underground outfit reeking of sweaty basements, not corporate highrises.

Stardog Records was in all effects an independent label created by Mother Love Bone to give their first release an indie feel.

The release party for *Shine* took place at the Oxford Tavern in Seattle. A few days later MLB flew to Boston for the first date of their tour: forty shows in total opening for Dogs D'Amour, a British hard rock band defined rather unflatteringly by one observer as an "eyeliner sporting quartet of Hanoi Rocks pretenders" [24], who were also signed to PolyGram and produced by Dearnley.

At first the two outfits got on like a house on fire, fueled by plenty of alcohol, although Dogs would fill their traditional pint glasses with wine, not beer.

Andy as usual was a source of entertainment and fun, especially in the long bus drives between performances, spent playing never-ending games of *Classic Football 2*. This especially helped ease tension if the show the night before had not exactly been stellar. But the tour was long and tiring, and gig after gig the relationship between the two bands soured.

It was soon obvious Mother Love Bone were vastly supe-

24 Definition taken from the book *Five Against One- The Pearl Jam Story*, by Kim Neely, Penguin Books, 1998.

rior to *Dogs*, and when the opening act is better than the headliner, there's gonna be trouble.

The mounting strain between the two outfits came to a head during one of the last stops of the tour, at the Whisky A Go Go in Los Angeles. *Dogs* took up almost the entire stage when they set up their instruments, leaving very little room for Mother Love Bone's opening set.

Luckily Andy had a cordless mic, and he solved the problem by singing in the middle of the audience, where he unequivocally expressed his opinion in the unbridled manner that characterized him.

"Those motherfuckers Dogs D'Amour can suck my dick!"

Backstage, among others, were the parents and fiancè of Bruce Fairweather, who in the meantime had gotten high on Robitussin DM, taken for a bad cough.

Despite the animosity that had developed with the headlining act, the tour was a success for Mother Love Bone. After passing the road test though, they were exhausted. They had a month and a half to recover, with no shows, just new songs to write, rehearse, rewrite, record.

The latter was done at Seattle's London Bridge Studios – where the band recorded a cover of *Hold Your Head Up* by the British band Argent. It was supposed to end up in a compilation by PolyGram of emerging bands covering tracks from the seventies. The compilation would never see the light of day, but that version of *Hold Your Head Up*, fine-tuned through countless hours in the studio, is a small masterpiece.

On July 28th 1989, following a month and a half of rehearsing five days a week, every week, for at least five hours a day, MLB played at Satyricon in Portland in what would be deemed one of the tightest performances of their brief career. Those hours of practice showed. The band had harnessed the chemistry that had always been there, but had not always fully manifested live on stage.

During that performance MLB played a song they had never played before.

It didn't have a definite structure, it didn't even have finished lyrics, Andy seemed to be going completely off the cuff, including giving the song an impromptu title.

"And now, ladies and gentlemen, this is *Portland Pussy Juice!*"

Nobody, not even Andy, could have imagined what lay in store for that song.

CHAPTER 22

BITE THE APPLE

"I remember my wife and I driving once, after a Mother Love Bone rehearsal, and we saw Andy walking down the street with his keyboard under his arm. We slowed down, and I said to him, 'Andy, rehearsal ended two hours ago. You're just now leaving?' He replied, 'Yeah, I stayed a little longer because I wrote another album.' That's the way he was. He was so prolific; he lived for it."

- Terry Date, Tape Op interview, by Jake Brown, 2018

Xana had a black eye and scratches on her neck.

Andy looked even worse.

When they got into a fight, it always got ugly. Xana's towering height allowed her to frequently get the better of Andy, but when he reacted, he'd give her a run for her money. Often when they visited David in Bainbridge they were blue and bruised, both inside and out.

Xana was finding it increasingly difficult to keep Andy on the straight and narrow; he had suffered a number of relapses since leaving the clinic. She would guard him like a hawk, but it wasn't enough. His addiction was getting out of hand.

Xana was convinced quitting was just a question of willpower, so the fact Andy lacked this quality irritated her tremendously. What also irritated her was the fact his habit was beginning to have an impact on their finances. She gave him money so he could buy what he needed, not to shoot drugs into his veins.

Things had further declined after the deal with PolyGram, which was the subject of choice during most of the dinners in Bainbridge. Xana had tried to make Andy's family understand that he was spiraling out of control, but nobody listened.

Yet she remained a safe harbor to him. He needed a place in the world where he could just be Andy, not the rock star everybody wanted to see, and that place was Xana. She was also the depository of his shame, of the deep self-loathing he felt for not being able to tame *the beast*. She was the one he ran home to, crying and begging her to save him until his eyes were swollen and rheumy. «I did it again. If you don't help me, I'll die», he would say. At first Xana would try to downplay things: "Don't worry babe, if you do it every once in a while, that's ok".

Every once in a while.

That's how little she knew about heroin.

Despite all her efforts, Xana was unable to get the message across to others. Most people thought she was exaggerating about Andy, especially the other members of Mother Love Bone. She was trouble, often appearing unannounced during rehearsals, taking Andy to one side where they would start arguing and fighting. The guys in the band wanted Xana out of the picture. And for a while she was; going to stay with her folks in Santa Fe, New Mexico, to get some space.

While this happened, PolyGram was shaping some big plans for Mother Love Bone; plans that would take Andy away from Seattle for a while. It was time to record their first album, at the glorious Record Plant Studios in Sausalito, California. A real institution in the world of rock music.

Founded in 1972 as a sister studio to the homonymous and older facilities in New York and Los Angeles, the Record Plant had generated legendary albums such as Fleetwood Mac's *Rumors*, an album that was notoriously recorded while at least two couples in the band were going through acrimonious and painful breakups.

At the mixing desk for Mother Love Bone's first full-length, by request of Kelly Curtis, was a familiar name: Terry Date, known in Seattle for his work with Metal Church, The Accüsed and Soundgarden (*Louder Than Love Lp*).

In the meantime, Mother Love Bone had acquired a sixth, unofficial member in the form of Denny Swofford, who went from being a diehard fan who taped and archived their gigs to an integral part of the band's entourage.

Denny had his own spot in Kelly Curtis and Susan Silver's office in Pioneer Square, and this allowed him to run into the two other bands under their management: Alice In Chains and Soundgarden. Three days a week Denny would be right there, handling the logistics of MLB's concerts and tours, replying to all the mail from their fan club, *Love Bone Earth Affair*.

Denny immediately made himself indispensable to the band, effectively solving many of the problems that most commonly afflict emerging outfits. He was the one in the driver's seat taking the group from one city to another for their shows for example.

Though he was a few years younger than Andy, Denny seemed the more mature of the two, both in spirit and attitude.

One of the first things Denny had noticed about Andy was his great ability as a communicator. He was able to skillfully direct any conversation, steering it away from topics he didn't want to discuss. Such as his addiction.

Originally from Portland, Oregon, Denny was well aware of the importance of Satyricon, one of the city's main clubs for live music, and a mecca for the rock scene. Mother Love Bone performed there twice: on May 3rd and September 6th 1989.

The next day after the second gig, they were on the road to Sausalito.

Andy Wood & Denny Swofford, Seattle's Central Tavern, 02/10/1989.
Photo by Jeff Betts
Courtesy of Cavity Search Records

Mother Love Bone entered the Record Plant as rookies, but honed by intense rehearsal sessions, full of optimism, and with a bunch of brand-new tunes. It wasn't easy to pick which ones to record in the studio, and not all the tracks they recorded ended up on the album.

One particular song, *Portland Pussy Juice*, the bizarre tune they had played their first time at The Satyricon, just wasn't working. The dissatisfaction each member felt towards it was palpable. It was a ballad with a simple structure that started with a riff from Stone's guitar, making it instantly recognizable from the very first notes. It had the potential to become a *good* song, but it had been suspended for months in a sort of limbo, with unfinished lyrics and a drum pattern Greg was having a hard time pinning down.

Even Andy, who had executed it for the first and last time at The Satyricon, didn't know what to sing.

«Fantastic», he had ironically remarked at the end of performing it.

For this and other reasons, that song, now known as *Dollar Short*, didn't make it onto the list of tunes to be worked on at the Record Plant.

The sessions began on April 12th 1989. The band, with Terry Date and Denny Swafford in tow, set up in two apartments inside a condo.

The first days of recording did not get off to a great start. The studio had been built in the seventies, so the drums were relegated to their own booth, with the rest of the band in the live room. Greg wasn't happy with how he sounded in that small, confined space. The furnishings also looked like they hadn't been updated since America had recorded *Hearts* there back in 1975.

The band was demoralized, and even debated whether to change studios. It took three days of trial and error to get the settings right and to everyone's satisfaction.

The recording process perfectly depicted the dynamics

between the various band members, as they always had been: Andy gladly delegated anything that didn't concern the music to Curtis and the others. Sometimes he would give his opinion on a take or a mix, but he mostly focused all his energies on recording the vocals. Jeff, who had always had an eye on the band's marketing and branding, acted as a bridge between Kelly and Andy.

Stone displayed maniacal attention to detail, going so far as to record fifty overdubs of the same guitar riff, without ever being happy with it. Usually that was when Greg stepped in. "Whaddaya mean you don't like it? It's the best thing you've ever done!".

Greg was without a doubt the most grounded member of the group, and though always very opinionated, he knew how to balance directness and diplomacy. Bruce had the gentlest temperament, it was really hard to pick a fight with him. The most heated arguments concerned the guitar and drums, the founding elements of the Seattle sound. Hours could be spent discussing a snare or a bass drum, or fiddling with the settings of the amps and effects pedals.

To make Andy more comfortable when he recorded his vocals, Date created a small alcove for him in a corner of the studio, with candles and a keyboard. Andy felt more at ease singing with his hands on a keyboard. Date also added a delay effect and reverb to his headphones, to mimic the effect of a live performance. Since the band was accustomed to playing medium-sized venues, that was the atmosphere he was trying to recreate.

Andy wrote all of the lyrics, he would have had a hard time trying to sing other people's words. His own words had mostly taken shape in the course of the previous year – a very complicated year. *Stardog Champion*, which PolyGram had picked as the first single, is almost a patriotic hymn. Even Andy didn't really know what the title meant, but it sounded good. The tune featured a children choir from the Bay Area, who took part in the recording sessions. For an entire day, for an entire day a horde of miniature singers took possession of the studio, creating an adorable chaos.

Come Bite The Apple is an almost autobiographical track, it's a sort of "invitation to sin, or not sin", but also a clear snapshot of Andy's state of mind at the time: someone who was conscious of being the saboteur of his own dreams.

In *Heartshine*, Andy expresses something that had been festering inside him for a long time but had remained unspoken: his guilt over abandoning Malfunkshun, and upsetting his brother Kevin's plans. Both Kevin and Brian jump out from between the lines of that song's lyrics.

Holy Roller's title was inspired by *Let Me Roll It* by Paul McCartney and Wings. The long instrumental bridge in which Andy freestyles took numerous takes in the studio before it came out right. The rest of the lyrics reflect the concept of *Loverock* that had been the guiding principle throughout Malfunkshun's existence.

This is Shangri-Là, the album's opening track, caused a lengthy discussion in the studio regarding the use of the reverse drum sample in the intro. Jeff and Stone hated it, but in the end it was included anyway. *Man of Golden Words*, a simple ballad with piano and keyboard, is a signature Andy Wood composition, celebrating the craft of songwriting and music as a universal language. And then there's *Stargazer*, practically the only song Andy ever composed with a guitar, usually all his music started with a keyboard.

Slowly but surely,the album was taking shape.

It would be titled *Apple*.

Andy & Stone @ Bumbershoot Festival, 09/03/1989
Photo by Todd Hottell. Courtesy of Cavity Search Records.

CHAPTER 23

Loma Prieta

"We were not happy as a band at that point. We were struggling with each other and stressed about making this record. I don't think it was a joyous time."

- Stone Gossard, interview with the author, 2015

San Francisco's Tower Records in Columbus Street was an institution. It opened in 1968 – what better time? – eight years after the main store in Sacramento. The sign read "Largest record store in the known world, open nine to midnight 365 days a year".

On October 17th 1989, Andy Wood, Denny Swofford and Greg Gilmore were at Tower Records, to kill the time in-between recording sessions for *Apple*. Greg had actually tracked all his drum parts in just five days, so he had plenty of time off. It *only* took an hour and a half by bike to go from Sausalito to San Francisco, with said vehicles being kindly provided by The Plant.

While some members were recording their takes in the studio, the rest of the band would ride to Frisco, and enjoy the splendid views from the Golden Gate Bridge. As long as nobody was throwing themselves off it, which sadly happened quite often at certain times of year.

That day at Tower Records, the boys were buying a movie to watch later in the evening. The routine that had developed after their recording sessions consisted in spreading themselves out on the couch of Bruce and Denny's apartment, in the company of the usual beers, a few joints, and some pizzas. The uniform always consisted of sweatpants, slides and dirty hair - Andy kept his swept up beneath his Dallas Cowboys cap.

All of them would be there chilling, except for Jeff, who would be busy on the phone with someone, discussing some detail of a song's arrangement he wasn't happy with.

On the first floor of Tower Records that day was a row of TV sets tuned into the Baseball World Series on ABC: Oakland Athletics versus San Francisco Giants. A close-up shot of Don Robinson's jersey faded into a bird's-eye view of the Bay, and a voice announced:

"I'm Al Michaels, welcome to Game Three..."

A small group of people had formed in front of the TVs, when suddenly there was static, then the screen went black. The agitated voices of the sportscasters could be heard speaking over each other before the audio signal also died. A green screen appeared with the words "World Series".

Andy and Denny were queuing at the cashier when an entire row of VHS tapes hit the floor like rapid-fire. The ground under their feet started shaking and a growing rumble could be heard in the distance, similar to an approaching thunderstorm.

"Fuck, an earthquake!», exclaimed Denny.

"Fuck, the circus!", thought Andy, wide-eyed at the prospect of witnessing the scenario that was about to unfold. He didn't really know what fear was, while at the same time being scared of so many things.

He noticed Greg on the lower floor bolting towards the exit, faster than Andy had ever seen him run. That wasn't a good sign.

A terrified and disordered crowd had gathered in the square near Tower Records, some were trying to call home from the phone booths, but all lines were disconnected.

In the meantime, at The Plant, Jeff, Bruce and Stone were taking a break, rolling joints and playing Galaga in the lounge area. Then suddenly the lights went off. The boys made their way down the winding corridor that opened onto the street: it was five in the afternoon, and everything was shaking. A group of terrified people ran out of the building and stationed at the entrance of the studios, convinced it was safer; others preferred the outdoor parking lot nearby.

Jim Gaines, at the time manager and resident sound engineer of The Plant, was in Studio A, in the process of recording the album *Spirits Dancing In The Flesh* by Santana.

Carlos Santana himself wasn't in the building (he was out shopping), but Gaines was recording some organ overdubs by Chester D. Thompson. That's when everything started shaking.

"What are you doing?", they asked each other at the same time, thinking the other was making the mixing desk quiver. When they realized neither was responsible for the movement, they rushed out of the studio, the floor undulating beneath them.

"Ok guys, I think we're done for today", Gaines stated matter-of-factly to the band when he met them outside. He opened his briefcase and took out a bottle of tequila, from which he and Thompson began taking sips, as they listened to the confusing news coming from the radio.

"The Bay Bridge is collapsing! The freeway is collapsing!"

The earthquake only lasted a handful of seconds, but it seemed like hours. Those few seconds were sufficient to take the lives of sixty-three people and crack the Bay Bridge in two. The outcome would have been even worse if the World Series hadn't been taking place, and traffic had been the usual at rush hour.

With a magnitude of 7.1 on the Richter scale, this earthquake would be known as "Loma Prieta", like the highest peak of the Santa Cruz mountains.

For three or four days there would be no electricity in most of the city. Everything at The Plant was at a standstill: a mixing desk had been seriously damaged; all the machines had to be recalibrated, and tapes realigned.

Even the phones were off. The only thing that was still functioning was the fax machine; nobody really figured why.

The members of Mother Love Bone, along with Terry Date and Denny Swofford, were forced to wait. For a few days, they all hunkered down in their apartments, listening to a battery-operated radio twenty-four hours a day, illuminated by candlelight at night. It was hard to sleep, and they couldn't even phone home.

Had it not been the outcome of dramatic events, this time-out would have been a welcome relief. After a month spent working on *Apple*, tensions in the studio had reached fever pitch. The amount of downtime between recording sessions was causing friction within the band. Greg had recorded all his drum parts in just five days, so his job was done.

Luckily Terry Date revealed himself to be a great team leader and an excellent mediator, attentive to everybody's needs and able to contain discontent, as far as that was possible. More importantly though, he had a great relationship with Andy. Date was fascinated by Andy's magnetic, almost boyish charisma, and the vocal attributes that placed him somewhere between David Lee Roth and Freddie Mercury.

One day as they were sitting together in the control room to re-listen to all the vocal tracks and decide which to keep and which to trash, Andy jolted up and ran towards the vocal booth. There was a fire under his keyboard. The candles he had lit during his recording session to create the right atmosphere had fallen to the ground and the flames had quickly spread. The whole studio could have burned down.

These kinds of distractions were common occurrences at The Plant. Some of them could be traced back to the guests of the other studios: Santana's crew for example often distributed Santana Brownies, laced with hash.

Then there was the infamous Halloween party set up by The Plant. For all the partying going on in Seattle, the guys of Mother Love Bone had never seen anything that could remotely compare: there were topless women and people wearing masks. Stone got so high he had to lay down on the floor and later wandered out of the apartment, not knowing who he was, stumbling around for hours in a compound that was miles away from the studio.

"It was one of those nightmare party scenarios where you should have left four hours earlier", he claimed, in the aftermath.

The *Apple* sessions in Sausalito lasted three months in total: a huge amount of time, mostly spent arguing about layering and tuning. It was not a joyous process.

And it wasn't even over yet.

CHAPTER 24

Relapse

«From my point of view, anytime you do heroin you can die».

- Steve Turner, Mudhoney, interview with the author, 2015

"The patient uses humor to downplay the severity of the situation".

That's what was written on Andy's evaluation form at Seattle's Saint Cabrini Hospital, where he had gotten his first taste of rehab.

Defusing drama with irony, even in the bleakest moments, was in fact one of Andy's most noticeable characteristics. It came naturally, requiring no effort on his part, and allowed him to skillfully deflect attention away from topics that were unpleasant. Especially if they would upset anyone.

On the way back from Sausalito, with the finished master of *Apple* now ready for mixing, it was Andy whose delicate balance risked being upset. Three months away from Xana had not helped their relationship, which had been rocky to begin with.

But there was good news in the Wood household: Kevin had become a dad. Him and his wife Vicky had welcomed a baby boy, Jasper.

There was going to be a party after the baptism that Andy wouldn't have missed for anything in the world. He liked being present at family gatherings, even if it was now an extended family.

Following the ceremony, all the guests congregated in

the picnic area, where Andy as usual held court, this time theatrically narrating an anecdote about Xana and a presumed flirtation with another guy. As he told the story he waved a note in the air, a message his alleged rival had written to her, which he had found by chance on the windshield. He concluded the performance by declaiming "I see the grim reaper coming to take me. It's the beginning of the end!" in a fake-dramatic tone, making everyone laugh.

The clown *has* to make people laugh, even when his own heart is bleeding.

The suspicion Xana was cheating on him had festered in Andy's mind for some time. Whether it was true or not, the idea itself devastated him. But nobody had to know.

For her part, Xana was the only person who realized the true extent of Andy's condition. She often thought back to an episode: Andy curled up on the floor of the bathroom, terrified, obsessively repeating the same words: "I saw my future, I was dead". It had taken place a few years earlier, on Kevin's birthday. He and Andy had taken acid, but Andy had had a bad trip, reducing him to that sorry state for at least eight hours.

He really thought he was going to die.

At the time Xana had not given the episode much thought, as she believed Andy was doing what everybody else was doing. But as time went on, relapse after relapse, she had grown acutely aware of the fact that Andy's drug use had gotten massive. Even though he tried to hide it.

The other members of Mother Love Bone weren't particularly worried. The fact that he slept in a parking lot like a homeless person when he didn't want to face Xana at home, was just standard practice. As was not hearing from him for three or four days.

Actually, Jeff couldn't really come to terms with Andy not asking for help. Why would he decide to sleep outdoors when he might just crash on the floor in Jeff's own flat.

They were good buddies, after all.

The time always comes though, when absences become prolonged, more frequent, harder to ignore. When behavior becomes bizarre and can only be explained in one way. At that point Kelly Curtis called a meeting with the whole band, including Andy, to convince him to go to rehab. An intervention, as they call it.

The same old "twenty-eight days".

But it had to be done. It was a delicate time for the band, primed for their big international debut, their first full-length *Apple* almost ready for release and a tour to follow.

Andy had to be clear-headed.

Jeff Ament, Bruce Fairweather, Greg Gilmore, Stone Gossard send a message to Andy in rehab: "We are waiting for you", Seattle, 1990
Courtesy of Toni Wood

Once again he acknowledged the severity of the situation, submitting to the care of Valley General Hospital in Monroe, northeast of Seattle.

This news was received with relief by the rest of the band. Finally, Andy was taking care of himself. "We'll go visit him", was the pithy consensus.

Only Stone was really worried. He'd known Andy the longest, and had seen this same story unfold two years earlier. While everyone else saw Andy as the catalyst for attention, the aspiring rock star that made everything seem possible, Stone had also seen Andy as a vulnerable kid who was not equipped to face the harshness of the world.

Andy was the leader in a band of alpha males, with each member pursuing his own taste of success. Now, a stone's throw from their big debut, with all eyes pinned on Mother Love Bone, the pressure he was under had increased exponentially, as had expectations.

Andy had enjoyed the creative freedom that had come with having a big budget, but now he was feeling like a cog in a mechanism that was crushing him. It wasn't fun.

The new rehab program included, among other things, meetings with relatives and members of his inner circle: parents, bandmates, girlfriend. Been there, done that. Once again, Andy was upbeat, finding grotesque humor in any situation.

One morning Toni went in to meet with Andy and his therapist, just the three of them, so the doctor could better understand the relationship between mother and son. Toni sat alone in a room for half an hour, without seeing anyone arrive. Finally a swarm of girls entered, took their seats, and started talking about their eating disorders. Toni was in the wrong room. Andy found it hilarious; it was so typical of his mom.

Xana also went to visit him. Officially, only on Thanksgiving. But in reality, every night, in secret. After work she would embark on the journey, an hour each way, just to sneak him a pizza through the window.

Greg, Bruce, Jeff and Stone only went to see him once, in agreement with the therapist. None of them really understood what it meant to be admitted to rehab, and most of all, what getting out would entail. None of them had ever been through it.

During the visit, Bruce began to realize how deep-rooted Andy's substance-abuse problem was. He had smoked pot for the first time at twelve, then came shrooms and acid, followed by alcohol, cocaine, and finally, heroin.

Greg, known for his caustic comments, informed Andy the band could easily go ahead even without him.

But what none of them expected and had even remotely considered, was what Andy told them. "If you want me to tour with you, there will be no alcohol involved. If you want to drink you can do it at a bar".

An imperative with no way out: a "clean" tour, for the sake of the frontman.

Not all of them took it well.

Mother Love Bone on the cover of The Rocket Magazine, April 1990

CHAPTER 25

The Veil of Addiction

"Last time I saw Andy was at a convenience store. We were hanging out on the grass and he had a big handful of gummy worms. We just sat and he said "this is my new drug".

- Chad Channing, interview with the author, 2020.

Patients at rehab centers are often asked to compile a journal recounting their first time and subsequent uses of each narcotic substance.

For Andy, who had never talked about his addiction in depth to anyone but Xana, this came as a welcome novelty.

With the same painstaking attention to detail with which he had transcribed pages upon pages of *Fantasy Football* years earlier, Andy minutely chronicled his various experiences with drugs throughout the years. It was an inexorable escalation that culminated with him where he was: in rehab, for the second time. Had they not been the footnotes to a tragic downward spiral into addiction, the comments he wrote in the margins might have elicited a smile.

«Great year for my adolescence!», Andy noted about 1978, the year he first smoked pot.

1980 was when he started going to keggers, often fertile grounds for one's first experiments with drugs.

From 1982 onwards it was a succession of «pot», «mushrooms», «(a lot of) acid», «alcohol», "MDA" "XTC", up to the turning point, 1988: the year heroin had stepped into the picture. The list then took on darker overtones. In the margins Andy recorded the most common side effects: "O.D.",

"Blackouts", and occasionally self-medicating with Percocet, an opioid used to relieve pain.

This road map ended at a crossroads: "1990 – one of two roads"[25], Andy wrote in the last chapter of his journal. In one direction life, in the other, death.

Everything seemed to indicate he had chosen life.

Out of rehab and one hundred days sober, Andy had turned a new leaf, and was politely declining beers in the backstage of Seattle Center Arena, where The Cult were about to perform. "That stuff is off limits for me!", he stated.

Andy adored The Cult, but that hadn't always been the case. It was music Xana liked, a bit like her affinity for The Cure. He often made fun of her for her taste in music, but in the end she had exercised her influence on him in this field as well.

When Robert Smith's band had played in Seattle, Xana had gone to see them alone; Andy was patiently waiting outside, sitting by the big fountain in Seattle Center. "Did you have fun?", he had asked her in a fatherly tone when she came out[26].

The Cult had already performed in Seattle during their tour of *Electric*. That time they had played at The Paramount and their opening act had been the newly-formed Guns N'Roses, L.A.'s most promising act and the band of Duff McKagan, who had returned to his hometown a star.

He had made it.

But there was another episode that had consolidated Andy's love for The Cult. It was during a Mother Love Bone show in Montreal while on tour with Dogs D'Amour, when Andy had been making his way among the audience with

25 From the "drug-a-log", written by Andy himself while in rehab, as quoted by Scot Barbour in *Malfunkshun, the Andrew Wood Story*, Universal /The Maze, 2005

26 Xana La Fuente, Xanaland, Grunge Storytellers, Mother Love Bone Meets Ian Astbury & The Cult: Love Blossoms in the Land of Thru Fade Away. grungestorytellers.xanaland.com/2013/07/mother-love-bone-meets-ian-astbury-cult.html#sthash.C8cTJq1x.dpuf

his cordless microphone, as usual. All of a sudden he had trotted back on stage like an excited puppy, and had whispered to his band members what he had discovered: Ian Astbury was in the audience.

Andy would never have imagined seeing him there.

So on January 4th 1990, when The Cult were in Seattle touring for their new album *Sonic Temple*, Andy just *had* to be there. That night, the cream of Seattle's musical crop was filling the lobby of The Seattle Center Arena: Andy, Stone, Jeff, Greg, but also Chris Cornell, with his manager and wife Susan Silver, and Jason Everman, who had briefly played second guitar in Nirvana (and would later, equally briefly, play bass in Soundgarden).

Chris Cornell, Andy Wood, Ian Astbury, Seattle Center Arena, 1989. Photo by Jesse Higman

In virtue of their shared record label – The Cult were also under PolyGram – Mother Love Bone were invited backstage, and the brotherhood was sanctioned with a group photo in the bathroom.

Andy and Ian immediately clicked, thanks in part to their shared experiences with addiction. Ian was also fresh out of rehab, only his problem was alcohol.

They spent much of that evening talking, finding solace in each other. Andy stayed on the tour bus for a while, studying a book Ian was reading, called *Witness to Fire: Creativity and the Veil of Addiction* by Linda Schierse Leonard, which explores the relation between creativity and addiction.

Before going on stage, Ian's girlfriend brushed his hair, slowly, for what seemed like hours.

Andy and Xana observed them, transfixed.

It's standard procedure once out of rehab to check in for weekly meetings that tackle any issues regarding the hardest part of the detox process: returning to everyday life.

In Andy's case it was Denny Swofford, "the man of many hats", who accompanied him to all his meetings. Those brief journeys by car represented precious glimpses into Andy's personal life, and Denny felt privileged to have access to that part of him. That part where Andy was only Andy, with his fears and his constant struggle to stay clean.

Denny was sharing an apartment with Bruce Fairweather in Wallingford, a neighborhood on a hill overlooking Lake Union, not far from downtown, between Fremont and the U-District.

You knew you were in Wallingford because of the enormous sign towering over the roof of its local indoor market. It was also full of Craftsman bungalows with low-pitched roofs and large porches, popular in the twenties. Denny and Bruce had chosen that area because rents were cheap, but most of all because the place they had found was right above a small store, Durn Good Grocery, which became Bruce's personal beer supplier. He didn't even have to cool it in the fridge, he just went downstairs, entered the store, bought a can, went back up and drank it on the sofa. It almost became second nature, often repeated numerous times a day.

Wallingford was also where Julia's Restaurant, an italian eatery, was located. It had a small outdoor area with a few tables decorated with kitsch plastic flowers. Michael David McCready,in his early twenties, who had moved to Seattle as a kid, worked there almost every day. Mike had been the guitarist in a band called Shadow, one of the most representative of the metal scene in Bellevue and the Eastside.

Shadow had tried their luck in L.A., where they had moved for a while in the hopes of landing a record deal, but nothing had happened, and they had returned to Seattle with their tails between their legs, to disband not much later.

Only a few years before that, Shadow had opened for Green River at Gorilla Gardens, right when punk and metal were finding a way to coexist, and hardcore bands were starting to slow down their tempo, with lasting effects on the scene.

Stone and Mike went way back. They had met in 1979, before Stone was in Green River and Mike in Shadow, at Madrona School in Seattle, where they used to trade music trading cards.

Mike had already picked up a guitar by then; Stone had not.

At Madrona Mike had also met Rick Friel, a fun-loving kid who carried his lunch in a Kiss lunchbox. They would later go on to form Shadow.

Now that Mike no longer had a band, he had cut his hair and had fallen into a state that closely resembled and preceded depression. He didn't like working at the restaurant, but he had to pay the rent somehow.

He had recently been dragged unwillingly to a party somewhere by a friend. With no desire to socialize, he had spent the entire night sitting on the floor next to the stereo, improvising guitar solos over an album by Stevie Ray Vaughan.

Stone Gossard had also been at that party and had observed him for some time.

That guy was an ace guitarist. How strange, that they had never played together.

CHAPTER 26

Party's over

"I was the druggie of the band.
Until I went to treatment".

Andy Wood, interviewed by RIP Magazine's
Michael Edward Browning, March 15th, 1990.

October 15th, 1979 had been a memorable day for Seattle's punk community, a date worthy of being etched in the brain. It was the day The Clash played at the Paramount Theatre, their first time performing in Seattle, with a lineup that had changed various times already since their formation. The show would leave an indelible mark (and in some cases permanent damage) on the eardrums of the attending public. The sheer volume made the theatre's sumptuous chandeliers quiver and sway from the ceiling.

Fast forward ten years, and The Clash were part of rock's pantheon: Joe Strummer had just released his new solo album *Earthquake Weather*, and was scheduled to perform at the Bacchanal in San Diego, with his band Latino Rockabilly War. It was November 21st 1989. At the drums was a guy named Jack Irons, borrowed from the Red Hot Chili Peppers.

It was one of Irons' first appearances following a lengthy break. The previous year RHCP had lost their guitar player and founder Hillel Slovak to a heroin overdose and it had hit Jack hard, resulting in a burnout that had pushed him to quit the band at the time. Only Strummer had been able to convince him to play again.

The backstage of the Bacchanal was full of stagehands loading and unloading equipment, mostly kids volunteering.

One of them stood out: he was wearing camouflage cargo pants, combat boots, had long hair swept up in a messy ponytail and moved in a slow, laid-back manner.

He didn't work at the Bacchanal regularly but it was like a second home to him. He loved hanging around and helping out, just to get free access to gigs, anything that would get him closer to the musicians he worshipped. Mainly because he was a musician too: he sang and played guitar in a local rock band called Bad Radio. When he had time, he also played drums in Hovercraft, his girlfriend's band.

He had joined Bad Radio three years earlier by responding to an ad in the paper. He had sent an audition tape of himself singing *Atlantic City* by Bruce Springsteen.[27]

His name was Eddie Vedder.

In a short amount of time he had not only become Bad Radio's chief songwriter, but for all intents and purposes their manager and artistic director. He booked their gigs, designed their artwork, kept in touch with radio stations and promoters.

Eddie wanted Bad Radio to be an activist band and had arranged for them to play at big local benefit events.

In spite of that, he was beginning to think he should leave the group. His ambitions were bigger than Bad Radio, bigger than San Diego, and bigger than the Chevron gas station where he had to work to make ends meet.

For most of his teenage years, Eddie's life had been a rollercoaster. Up to the age of fifteen, "dad" had been the man his mom was married to. Then one day she had come out with the horrible truth, and had revealed that his real father was actually the family friend who would come by every once in a while, and who had just died of multiple sclerosis. This meant the man they lived with, Mr. Müller, a guy Eddie didn't really get along with, had no relation to him whatsoever.

It had come as a complete shock to Eddie, but deep down, it was not totally unwelcome news. Ever since he was a kid he

27 John Colapinto, *Eric Boehlert and Matt Hendrickson, Eddie Vedder: Who Are You?*, Rolling Stone n.748

had always feared becoming "Mr. Normal", like the man in *We're Not Gonna Take It* by The Who, and up to that point his life had pretty much gone in that direction.[28]

His mom eventually moved to Chicago with his younger brothers, but Eddie stayed in California, namely Encinitas, a beach city in the North County area of San Diego. His adolescence had been a place of solitude and premature responsibility. At just fifteen, he'd had to quickly learn to fend for himself, and had started working at a drugstore to pay his bills.

He later moved to La Mesa, a tropical paradise of sand and sea close to San Diego. The perfect place to surf, one of his passions, and also to focus on the guitar, his other great love.

Just like his real father, who Eddie had eventually found out had also been a singer and a musician, and had even recorded some tracks.

That night at the Bacchanal was when Eddie and Jack Irons met for the first time and it would prove to be a difficult night. A few minutes into Strummer's set, the opening band shut down the venue's power over a dispute on their fee. Eddie led everyone backstage with his flashlight and held it for Strummer as he rolled a joint.

That moment marked the beginning of Eddie Vedder and Jack Irons' friendship, a bond that would be more significant than either could have imagined at the time.

In November of 1989 Vedder wasn't the only one growing increasingly dissatisfied with his band. Over in Seattle, so was Andy. He often repeated something to his mother when he visited her in Bainbridge Island: once he reached the peak of success he would retire from performing and focus on composing movie scores.

The last time he had said this to her had been while they were at the laundromat. He was wearing tiger-print leggings, a cherry red t-shirt and a pair of high top sneakers. All the

28 Eddie Vedder, *The Howard Stern Show interview*, November 2nd, 2020.

women waiting for their laundry had turned and stared at him as if he were an alien.

"Will you also change your pants?", Toni had asked.

"I doubt it", was his reply.

In the meantime, having pitched the idea to PolyGram who had expressed an interest, Andy was working on a solo album, and wanted Kevin to be part of the project. Andy was living with Xana at the Marqueen Apartments, on Queen Anne Hill; a historic building which used to be the home to the Seattle Engineering School, and housed Henry Ford's students.

Kevin had already been there a few times, just to brainstorm and try out some ideas. Andy believed this would be the perfect opportunity to mend the rift between them and iron out any unresolved issues relating to Malfunkshun.

Though he didn't want to admit it, Andy wasn't happy with Mother Love Bone. The band could guarantee him a certain level of notoriety, but it didn't give him the outlet he needed to become the best performer and songwriter he could be. There was something diabolical in the bizarre mechanism that was sucking him in. What was he supposed to do with the dozens of songs he had written? And was the path that had been mapped out for Mother Love Bone right for him?

In the meantime, *Apple* was ready to be mixed and mastered at Sound Castle Studios in Los Angeles with British producer Tim Palmer, who could boast a vast array of collaborations, from pop sensations Cutting Crew or Dead Or Alive, to Robert Plant or David Bowie's Tin Machine.

Palmer had been hand-picked by the band's manager, Michael Goldstone, who was the only one present in the studio to follow the process. For the first time in his career, Palmer wasn't working in conjunction with the band he was mixing. He only had a few phone conversations with Jeff, Stone and Kelly Curtis.

A few minutes into his first listen of the album, Palmer had immediately realized Andy had rock star potential. He also appreciated the various influences emanating from the band: there was definitely a dominant rock component, but also something experimental and unexpected in the songs.

At the end of Palmer's work, *Apple* was a much more polished album than it had been when it had exited the Plant and left Terry Date's hands. "Spacey, and weird sounding", was how Andy defined it in an interview with Michael Edward Browning of *City Heath* a few months later. He also added that Date probably wouldn't approve of how his creation had been transfigured.

It took seven months to complete this final stage of the process. As many as five or six tracks had required a completely new mix.

The end result included all the tracks that had been recorded at the Plant except for one, *Seasons Changing*.

Finally, the countdown to the much-awaited promotional tour of the album could begin. Forty-eight dates in as many American cities, with Raging Slab from New York as the opening act. Denny started making hotel reservations, and packing his bags.

Before that though, Mother Love Bone had a few local gigs. On January 3rd 1990 they performed at the Vogue, and Andy announced the birth of Jessica, Kelly Curtis and his wife Peggy's first child. "The baby has black skin: I don't know how that could have happened", he joked on stage, as always.

After an encore playing covers of *Hold Your Head Up* by Argent and *I'm in Love With My Car* by Queen, Andy thanked Green River for breaking up and giving him "my guys". He then reminded the audience to drive safe and go straight home "cause it's Wednesday", and the next day was a work day.

On March 9th 1990 Mother Love Bone performed at the Central, for the last show before the official launch of *Apple*.

It would be their last show ever.

Bruce Fairweather, Denny Swofford, Greg Gilmore, Seattle's The Oxford, 02/10/1989. Photo by Jeff Betts
Courtesy of Cavity Search Records

Stone Gossard, Denny Swofford, Jeff Ament, Seattle's The Oxford, 02/10/1989. Photo by Jeff Betts
Courtesy of Cavity Search Records

Denny Swofford & Andy Wood, Halloween Party, November 1989, The Plant Sausalito, Ca. Courtesy of Denny Swofford

Denny Swofford & Andy Wood, proto- selfie, November 1989, The Plant Sausalito, Ca.
Photo by Andy Wood
Courtesy of Denny Swofford

PART 4

CHAPTER 27

This pink cloud

"My brother was concealing a very dark secret. And nobody knew until it was too late."

- Kevin Wood, interview with the author, 2015

Andy was flashing his brightest smile while talking to Michael Edward Browning for an article on *RIP* magazine. It wasn't the first time their paths had crossed. Less than a year earlier Browning had seen Mother Love Bone perform at the Oz Nightclub in Seattle, and had penned a concert review. Actually, it had been the very first piece he had submitted to the magazine, and he wasn't even sure they would publish it.

That night at the Oz, Mother Love Bone were sharing the bill with Alice in Chains, and Andy had done voice soundcheck for Layne Staley, so he could rest his voice. As he couldn't remember the words to their song *I Know Something*, Andy made up the lyrics, making everyone laugh.

At the end of their set, Mother Love Bone performed a cover of *I'm In Love With My Car* by Queen, except with one small variation. The hook was changed to "I'm In Love With Mike Starr", as a playful reference to Alice in Chains' bass player.

Months later Browning saw Mother Love Bone perform again at Legends in Tacoma, a show where everybody in the audience competed for the biggest hair.

On that occasion he had exchanged a few words with Andy and Greg, a few feet away from the stage, with music blasting at full volume from the speakers around them.

Andy had confessed to him that he was in no rush to go on tour, he needed time to get back on his feet after rehab. The rest of the band, on the other hand, couldn't wait.

Now being interviewed by Browning in an official capacity, Andy was just as candid. He wasn't like other musicians who were averse to talking to the press and fans. The conversation touched on all the crucial moments that had accompanied Mother Love Bone's rapid ascension: releasing *Shine*, the difficult tour with Dogs D'Amour, signing with PolyGram, recording *Apple*.

All in just over two years.

They discussed the nerve-wracking buildup that preceded MLB finally signing to PolyGram, and Andy remarked it was worth the wait: «I was psyched, cause of course [Geffen] was the *hip* label at the time. Then it was like, we are waiting forever for them to do something. And then PolyGram got to the point. PolyGram's got cooler bands. AND Neil Young hated Geffen, so...», he trailed off.

Browning's next question was by no means obvious.

"Did MLB loose any of its *grunge*?"

"I don't know. Did we have any grunge in the first place? I guess there's still a little grunge in the guitars from the Green River days. We didn't lose any of the grunge we needed, but we may be right in throwing some of the ugly grunge away. It's called 'stale grunge'".

In 1990 the term "grunge" didn't designate a musical genre or youth culture yet. "Grunge" had first made its appearance in the music scene just three years prior, in one of the very first catalogs of Sub Pop Records, compiled by Bruce Pavitt himself. In it he had described Green River's album *Dry As A Bone* and the label's compilation *Sub Pop 100* as "ultra-loose grunge that destroyed the morals of a generation".

Browning then asked what format *Apple* would be released on, and Andy replied that the label were planning to release the album on CD and cassette, but the band were insisting it come out on vinyl as well. "Many of our fans don't have a CD player" – he noted, adding that PolyGram could license an external distributor to press vinyl copies. "And with each record, a free pair of underwear!", Andy joked, "Xana has so many".

Xana, of course, was there with him, talking over everybody to someone on the phone. Andy didn't go anywhere without her.

At this point Browning took out some photos he had shot of Mother Love Bone's show at Legends. "I wanted some more pics to accompany the interview, maybe you have some?", he asked. That was Xana's cue to cut in, waving a series of snapshots of a recent gig at The Vogue, taken by local photographer Paul Hernandez.

Andy's posture stiffened.

"Why haven't I ever seen these pictures before Xana?" – he enquired with annoyance, but not anger.

"You said you didn't want to see them".

Simple.

"Please remember to mention the photographer!", they both instructed.

What followed was a risky digression on the various music magazines in the Pacific Northwest and their alleged rivalry. Andy felt like *Backlash* was the magazine for hip kids and *City Heat* was for losers. "I'm not gonna name names, but some bands seem very concerned with the quality of their fans", he observed.

Andy wasn't interested in that kind of dynamic. He wanted his audience to be equally interested in a Mudhoney concert as, say, in a Talks Cheap show.

He also commented with some indignation on the fact Green River had *never* been on the cover of a magazine in spite of being one of the most influential bands of the Seattle sound.

Andy then spoke about his role in the band: "For now I'm the only one writing lyrics, but I don't consider myself a songwriter" - he explained. "I consider myself someone who writes songs. I don't even know how to read music: I never tell the others: 'give me a C, give me an E'. They listen to me and play what needs to be played".

Mother Love Bone @ Legends, Tacoma, WA, 01.26.1990
Photo by Todd Hottell. Courtesy of Cavity Search Records.

To conclude the interview, Browning dared to enquire about the band's vices: who used what.

Andy had no hesitation in opening up about his past struggles and revealed that, before going to rehab, he was «the druggie of the band».

He thought the rest of the guys were boring. How did they even have fun without getting high?

"We've got people who drink in the band, people I don't doubt are alcoholics - and I don't think they doubt it either" Andy stated. "But luckily there was no one really into pot or any other drugs as much as I was. So I don't have to deal with those guys staying stoned, although I don't do it anymore. They're happy with their beers" he continued, "But the day Bruce stops drinking beer is the day monkeys fly out of my butt, like in *Wayne's World*".

In various instances Andy repeated he had been clean for months, and wasn't using anything.

«I'm lucky to be sitting here», he stated matter- of-factly, when asked about his recent monthlong stay in rehab, which still involved attending weekly follow-ups every Monday night. Still it was a total struggle. «When you first get out, you're on this pink cloud, and it's pretty easy", Andy confessed openly. "After a while things start getting more real, and you have to just stay straight a second at a time».

Staying straight meant not stopping at every corner in Seattle where there was always someone ready to remind him about what he still craved.

At that point, it was time for Browning to wrap up the interview. Andy and Xana had to drive to Tacoma, where Aerosmith were scheduled to play a gig in the evening. They wouldn't have missed that show for anything in the world.

It wouldn't have been too far-fetched to imagine Love Bone opening for Aerosmith at some point in the near future.

CHAPTER 28

Goodbye, just in case

"We [Mudhoney] had just come back from the Australian tour. I remember Jonathan Poneman met us at the airport and we thought, like 'This is weird'. He had never met us at the airport before. 'Guys I have some bad news for you' he said. 'Andy Wood is in a coma at the hospital, and it looks like he's not gonna make it". It was horrible. Felt bad for everybody involved."

-Mark Arm, interview with the author, 2015

"Hey man, I'm not feeling that good, I'm not coming. I trust your decision, whatever it will be."

Andy's voice on the phone was hoarse and a bit nasal, as if he had a cold.

An important meeting was supposed to take place at Kelly Curtis' office. It was with a potential tour manager for the band, a man who was well-versed in matters of musicians with addiction issues.

In the last few months Andy had been working out with Jeff at the gym everyday in preparation for Mother Love Bone's upcoming tour. He had probably caught something in the locker rooms, the other band members assumed. Truth was, Andy hadn't even gone to the gym that day.

Meanwhile, PolyGram's mighty marketing machine had kicked in full gear: Mother Love Bone had just done a shoot for what would probably be the cover of *Apple*, with a guest appearance by Jessica, Kelly Curtis' newborn.

MLB, Apple Photoshoot, 1989
Photo by James Bland.

Andy had been clean for almost a hundred days. So he said, at least. Those who knew him well knew he was struggling, trying to stay sober and keep up with life. He hadn't lost his ability to temper sadness with humor, but something inside him was broken.

Someone swore they saw him in a grocery store one day looking spaced out and lonely.

Around that same time, his brother Brian was passing by Pike Place one afternoon and had noticed a swarm of girls in the middle of the street. As he got closer, he saw what they were crowding around: his brother Andy, signing autographs. And looking miserable. Their gazes met, but Brian walked away. That had probably disappointed Andy.

The day of the meeting with the tour manager also happened to be a hellish day for Xana. Lately there had been various thefts in the store she worked at, and the boss had called a staff meeting and given them a good tongue-lashing. As if that weren't enough, she had to drive a few of her co-workers home, to the other side of town. It was great being the best and most appreciated staff member, but it came loaded with responsibilities.

When Xana finally got home it was 10pm. She went straight to the bedroom and saw Andy face-down on their bed.

Was he sleeping already?

"Babe?"

"Babe".

"LANDREW!".

She tugged at him.

Drug paraphernalia was lying at the foot of the bed, which quickly brought the picture into focus.

Xana dropped her bag, flung herself on Andy and checked his arms.

Her throat clenched. She couldn't even scream.

She called 911 in a panic, and then she *did* scream. So loud her neighbors on the floor above heard.

"Is he conscious?"

"No"

"Follow my instructions while the ambulance arrives. Can you do CPR?".

Only twenty-one years old, and she was being asked to perform a life-saving procedure.

The ambulance arrived quickly. The paramedics intervened on Andy while Xana stood by the door, in shock. Next thing she knew, Andy was lying in the Intensive Care Unit of Seattle's Harborview Medical Center, a myriad of tubes connecting him to various machines with blinking monitors.

Hospitals had been unwelcome recurring elements throughout Andy's short life.

Toni had a number of memories related to them, some of which were hilarious. She would often recall, for example, a funny episode that had happened decades earlier in Bremerton when Andy was still a child. They had gone to see their family physician, Dr. Mean (that was his *real* name) for the rashes Andy experienced due to his allergies. As they were leaving the ward, they had met a woman they knew by face only. She stopped them and was saying something, but Toni was lost in thought and dismissed her quickly by replying: «Oh, that's great!».

As they walked away, Andy looked at Toni and went: «Mom, that lady just told you her husband has died. And you said it was great».

Toni was mortified, and ran back to apologize.

Andy had laughed heartily. So much comedy there.

Now, at Harborview, her boy was no longer laughing. His life was, once again, in danger.

The tragic news of Andy OD'ing reached Jeff Ament as he'd just gotten back home at round 11pm. Someone had left a note on the door of his apartment: "Hey, I think your singer's in trouble". Even from outside he could hear the answering machine wildly beeping from all the messages Xana had left. She was hysterical, "They've taken him to Harborview, come quickly!"

But it was Toni and Kevin who arrived first.

Kevin had recieved a call at round three in the morning and had rushed to his mom, banging on her door.

"Mom. Andy overdosed. We gotta go."

"Is he gonna die, Kevin?", she dared ask.

"Don't even say that", he promptly replied.

Once at Harborview, they both sat in the waiting room for hours. They would not be allowed into intensive care while the medical staff tried to stabilize Andy.

The situation was that, while he may survive the heroin overdose, his brain activity might have been seriously compromised.

By around 6.30 am, Toni had fallen asleep. At this point, something weird happened.

Behind her was a window. Outside it was raining heavily. She suddenly heard a faint ticking sound, as if someone were knocking on the glass pane.

It was Andy.

"Mom, I'm out of my body, I just want you to know I might not be able to get back, I might have to say goodbye". Toni woke up suddenly, in shock, and shared the news with Kevin. "Andy is out of his body", she annouced.

"Oh, shut up mum."

Kevin did not believe that kind of narrative.

As crazy as it may have sounded, it made perfect sense to Toni, though. Andy would have tried to warn her, that he was gonna leave.

Andy had always had an obsession for souls leaving bodies, ever since he was a kid. "Mom, while I was praying last night I felt myself expand," he told her once. "I had an out-of-body experience!", he exclaimed dramatically, making her laugh.

At some point, at Harborview, Toni and Kevin were finally granted access to Andy's room. Toni stared at him silently. She thought he looked like a prince: he lay there quietly with his toenails polished – Xana had probably done that to him, back at home.

The nurses announced they would monitor Andy's brain activity for the next twenty-four hours, progressively reducing the medication that was keeping him in an induced coma.

Toni felt a sliver of hope. She went home thinking that maybe – yes, there might still be someone in there, in that beautiful body.

In a bizarre twist of fate, the night before the hospitalization, Kevin had dreamt Andy was having a relapse. He had called him in the morning. Andy had reassured him: "Hey, don't worry, I'm totally fine".

Toni headed back to Harborview the following morning at 5 o'clock. She wanted to be there by the time the doctors checked on Andy's brain activity after stopping the medication. Nobody had arrived yet. Some unknown lady came out of nowhere, grabbed Toni and kissed her on her cheek. She had no idea who that lady was, and never would.

"When the rest of the family is here, we will talk to you", the physician solemnly announced.

A bunch of people arrived soon after. Kevin, Xana, and Andy's long time friend Joe Abrams with his wife.

In the meantime, the news of Andy OD'ing had spread among the local music community. Denny Swofford had the worst task: he had to break it to Bruce, who had been away for a short vacation on Orcas Island.

For hours Denny waited for him in the dark, sitting on the sofa at their Wallingford flat.

When Bruce entered, he found Denny with an expression on his face he had never seen before.

"It's about Andy".

He didn't have to say anything else, Bruce understood.

He and Greg had often talked about Andy, the way he was handling the rehabilitation process, how he lived his life in such a fragile balance. But Bruce hadn't expected this tragic outcome. Not so soon.

An unusual crowd, nervously pacing back and forth, progressively populated the second floor of Harborview Medical Center; strange characters that had nothing to do with Andy stood in the hallways like birds of ill omen. In fact, not all of them were there for him.

The word going around was that other people had come in like him that same night, victims of what they call "a bad batch". Maybe from the same dealer, from the same streets, where lives cross paths with other lives before destiny calls.

In a twisted series of events, that very evening, before getting home, Andy had met Mike Starr of Alice In Chains in Kelly Curtis' apartment. It had been a surreal dialogue.

"Whats's up Andy? How ya doin?", Mike had asked.

"I got forty days clean, man".

"What the fuck does that mean?"

"Clean off heroin". [29]

They chatted for a while and then Mike gave Andy a lift home. Except he didn't get off at the MarQueen Apartments: he stopped Mike a few blocks from his place. "Just drop me off right here", he said. And walked up to a Mexican guy he knew.

Who knows if he went home alone to shoot up his dose. Or if someone was with him and ran off when things started to look bad.

Who knows what pushed him to get off two blocks too early, and choose that path of no return.

A path that would lead to a terrible verdict.

"Hypoxic ischemic encephalopathy".

The doctor informed the little crowd at Andy's bedside that his brain had swollen during the night, and showed no

29 Mark Yarm, *Everybody Loves Our Town, A History Of Grunge*, Faber & Faber, 2011, p. 229

signs of neurological activity. The situation was irreversible. It was the family's choice as to when to pull the plug.

That's when Toni's world fell apart. By hearing *that* word.

"Irreversible."

Xana, who was in charge at that point, and took all the decisions, informed everyone she wouldn't let them switch off Andy's life support until Chris Cornell, currently on tour with Soundgarden, but on the way back to Seattle, had arrived and said goodbye.

At 3:15 pm on March 19th 1990, Andy's heart stopped beating.

All meters slowly settled on zero.

Flat line.

The end.

Less than two weeks away from the release of *Apple*.

CHAPTER 29

He came from an island. And he died from the street

«Andy wasn't the Keith Richards of Seattle».

- Jeff Ament, Hard & Heavy interview, 1990.

Soundgarden's *Louder Than Love* tour had gotten off to a bad start.

Unhappy with his role in the band, bassist Hiro Yamamoto had quit and enrolled back in college. He was quickly replaced by Jason Everman, the guy who had briefly played guitar in Nirvana, and, most notably, lent them the money that was needed to record the *Bleach* sessions. He'd never gotten that money back, but Kurt Cobain credited him in the album.

The *Louder Than Love* tour had ended even worse than it had begun. Right after the last gig in Hoboken, New Jersey, Chris Cornell and Susan Silver flew back to Seattle and rushed to Harborview, where Xana was waiting for them with Andy on life support.

Chris was shortly due to fly to Europe for the second leg of the tour, both a blessing and a curse. It would be good to get away from Seattle during that time of grieving. He had just lost one of his best friends. Then again, he wouldn't be allowed time to grieve.

The image of Andy in that hospital bed, bloated and unrecognizable, would accompany him all through the tour and would haunt him for a long time after that.

He couldn't help blaming himself. He regretted not being able to save Andy, not being able to do *something*. He couldn't handle the awful feeling of emptiness. How could two human beings share such a connection and then have it severed so suddenly? How could two guys create a song like *Island Of Summer* and no longer be in each other's lives?

But most of all, how could Andy choose to go, with a whole new world of fame and opportunities waiting for him just around the corner? Because it had been *his* decision, right?

There was a period of time, as they were flatmates in the Melrose Avenue flat, when Andy would engage in this routine of dueling four-track demos and songs. Andy wasn't doing it for Malfunkshun and Chris was not doing it for Soundgarden; it had nothing to do with that. It was the two of them just having fun. They were always kind of neck and neck.[30]

Andy had never spoken openly to Chris about his addiction. In fact, he had done all he could to hide it. He was afraid it would make Chris love him less.

In Andy's eyes, Chris was the perfect example of someone who could keep it together. He had control of his life. He was the engine of his band. He had a day job, he had a dog and he could pay his bills.

Chris *had* found his place in the world. That's what Andy knew.

What he didn't know was that Andy himself was the reason Chris had found his place in the world. Even more so after Andy's death.

Only a few hours after Andy's passing, a congregation of musicians and friends had gathered in a spontaneous wake at Kelly Curtis' place. Curtis' close friend, movie director

30 Excerpt from: *Chris Cornell Talks Missing Andrew Wood, Writing Songs In the Bathroom: Unpublished 2015 Interview Excerpts*, Katherine Turman, Billboard, 05/19/2017, in the aftermath of Chris Cornell's death.

Cameron Crowe and his wife Nancy Wilson, also joined.[31]

Despite the grief, that was the first time Chris felt he was really part of something. He belonged to that city, to that community, to that mourning.

At one point in the wake, Layne Staley from Alice In Chains had entered the room and burst into tears. He cried for about an hour, but for some reason, nobody went to console him.

Then the ridiculous memorial service at the Paramount had taken place. Hundreds of people had stormed in from every suburb of Seattle. To some, it had looked more like a gloomy carnival parade than a memorial ceremony, totally inappropriate. Several people, including some who were really not entitled to it, felt the need to go on stage and give a speech.

David Wood also took the mic at one point. "If you gotta get another singer, don't get a junkie", he declared. Those words upset various people in attendance.

When Andy had wished he would "sell out the Paramount", he surely had not meant *this*.

Once back on tour with Soundgarden, Chris Cornell couldn't push away the pain. No matter where he went, it was right there with him. The only way he could tame it was by writing songs for Andy.

He started recalling the times he had seen him on stage, commanding attention, being master of the crowd. The way he had reached down to the audience and elevated it.

"Reach down / and pick the crowd up".

There it was.

The first song for Andy.

---

31 In a moving 1992 Rolling Stone article, Cameron Crowe explained why that gathering was a turning point for a script he was working on at the time, which ended up being the script for the cult Seattle-based movie *Singles. https://bit.ly/3gg4akM*

Seattle's Paramount Theatre celebrates Andy Wood

While Chris was looking for ways to process his grief, the surviving members of Mother Love Bone had another issue. What were they going to do with *Apple,* an album that had imploded before it was even released?

It was good and ready to go, but the band was no more.

The people at PolyGram were very understanding, and gave the remaining members of MLB all the time they needed to figure out what to do. The label had been eager for them to get a record out ever since signing them. But after Andy's passing, and with the mounting buzz surrounding the band, they were even more determined to release it. Ultimately, so were the surviving band members.

They had spent the last two years making that album, and something had to come of it.

Aside from the shared and unenviable task of grieving Andy, the end of Mother Love Bone meant something different to each guy in the band. Bruce Fairweather was overwhelmed. The end of that experience meant missing a further opportunity to travel the world making music, even though he knew they wouldn't have lasted another four years. To Greg Gilmore, the most rational of the group, losing a frontman didn't necessarily have to mean calling it quits. At the end of the day, Andy had made his choice, and it didn't have to affect the others. Mother Love Bone could go on with another singer.

He was alone in this sentiment.

To Jeff Ament, it meant another grinding halt on the verge of an achievement. It just seemed like every time his life was taking a right turn something would happen to knock it off course. His fate, he thought, was the same as that basketball team that's just about to win the season, and then suddenly the coach gets axed.

For this and other reasons, he had never given up his day job at Raison d'Être, serving espresso for five bucks an hour.

To Stone Gossard, the end of his band was a point of no return. Having known Andy for the longest time, his death was no surprise. He knew Andy had been clean and sober for the last couple of months, and he had felt reassured by the fact he was starting to take care of himself. Andy worked out on a daily basis, and seemed very focused on his music. He must have written around fifteen songs in the last four months.

Nonetheless, having known a number of addicts, Stone knew that just because a junkie stayed clean for four months, it didn't mean he was out of danger.

He also knew that Andy had this tragic flaw, a sensitivity that fueled his creativity on one hand but tormented him on the other. Stone knew that most of Andy's songs came from his inability to understand his own feelings, and the use of drugs was a byproduct of that confusion.

Apple was eventually released on July 19th 1990, through PolyGram/Mercury/Stardog Records, with no fanfare at all.

Stardog Champion got picked as the first single. A video was made, directed by a friend of the band, videomaker Josh Taft, who used archival live footage.

With no tour and just some t-shirts designed by Jeff as merch, the video was helpful to get some promo going.

To their great displeasure, Jeff and Stone had to spend some time in Los Angeles doing interviews.

"We still haven't really made a lot of decisions as far as to what context the band is gonna go on. It's definitely not gonna be called Mother Love Bone", Jeff stated in an interview for *Rock & Heavy* magazine, in the summer of 1990.

The band would take a break and let things happen naturally.

There was no rush to be rock stars at this point.

Once back from L.A., it was downtime for everybody. Jeff and Stone spent whole days biking around Discovery Park, taking a break at Westlake Fountain every once in a while. No music on their minds whatsoever. They just talked, reminisced, cried.

In spite of his resolve to never be a musician again, Stone soon found himself inevitably drawn back to his guitar. Snippets of songs started flowing unstoppably from his head again. For once, the guy who had control over everything, had no control. He would improvise riff after riff, taping them on cassette, labeling them "Riff 1", "Riff 2"...

He had reverted back to his old self as an undisciplined kid at North West School, deconstructing and experimenting with songs.

At that point, he did what he thought was the right thing to do.

He called his fellow guitarist Mike McCready.

CHAPTER 30

Humbly – but with some balls

"The Temple Of The Dog project was a very healing process in which all of those musicians and friends closest to Andy were able to mourn and celebrate the best and only way they knew how. I could tell that there was an important act of unspoken closure that came from those songs."

- Dave Abbruzzese, in conversation with the author, October 2016

Eddie Vedder had barely been in Seattle an hour. "Let's not fuck around, let's head straight to the studio", he announced to Jeff and Stone upon meeting them for the first time at Seattle-Tacoma Airport. No arrogance or bossiness intended; just a genuine desire to get to work.

He would get his wish. Eddie would soon be acquainted with the Belltown neighborhood in downtown Seattle, an area where, according to locals, "pigeons outnumber people most days". He was brought to a shabby basement studio everyone referred to as 'The Potatohead Gallery', taking its name from the art studio at the front of the building, on Second Avenue. It was a shithole crammed with guitars, drums, and amps strewn on threadbare carpets, with wires everywhere, and sheets and blankets tacked to the ceilings and walls for better acoustics. Posters of basketball players and guitar god Stevie Ray Vaughan hung on the walls as a source of inspiration for the band that jammed there.

A band called Temple Of The Dog.

Eddie couldn't stay long in Seattle - barely a week - then he had to fly back to La Mesa, near San Diego, in time to cover his graveyard shift at a Chevron petroleum warehouse.

The chain of events that had brought Eddie to Seattle unfolded rapidly and magically. In one of their multiple stints in L.A. for the promotion of *Apple*, Jeff and Stone had gathered the courage to call Jack Irons, former drummer of Red Hot Chili Peppers, and asked him to meet up. Having known him for some time, they were hoping he would join the band they were putting together.

Unfortunately, he had to decline, as he was going on tour with California punk band Redd Kross. Plus, he was about to become a dad.

Not wanting to miss an opportunity, the guys had handed him a demo with five instrumental songs that Stone and Jeff had recorded with guitarist Mike McCready and Seattle drummer Matt Cameron.

After Andy's passing, Stone had been the only former member of Mother Love Bone to write music more or less consistently. He and Mike McCready had rehearsed his new songs in the attic of his parents' house in Capitol Hill. Gossard had started making plans for a new band, but, surprisingly, those plans did not initially include Jeff Ament. After spending so much time together in the aftermath of Andy's death, they had somehow drifted apart. McCready had been instrumental in bringing Jeff back into the picture, convincing Stone to involve him in his new project. Stone had then booked some studio time at Jack Endino's Reciprocal Studios, for what would later be dubbed "The Gossard Demos sessions". The result was a dozen instrumental songs that sounded completely different to the Mother Love Bone formula; they were sultry, with downtempo patterns that melted into proper songs.

The tape Stone and Jeff eventually handed Irons had five of those tunes; five instrumental tracks just waiting for a singer. When Irons heard them, he instantly connected the dots: Eddie's voice would fit those gems perfectly.

He and Eddie had hung out frequently since meeting at

Joe Strummer's gig at the Bacchanal, so it was only a matter of time before he could hand him the tape.

In the early hours of September 13th 1990, Eddie Vedder pressed "play" on his car's cassette player. He listened to those songs over and over, on repeat, throughout the three hour drive from Los Angeles to San Diego, and all through his night shift at the gas station.

At 8 am, he clocked out, stowed his surfboard in the back of his black pickup truck, and hit Pacific Beach.

The music rolled in his head like waves as he surfed. Issues from his adolescence resurfaced and lyrics began to coalesce in his mind. By the time he got out of the water, three melodies and respective sets of lyrics were taking shape. He raced to his girlfriend's place near Mission Beach, fearing the words might slip away if he didn't commit them quickly to paper. Still wet from his surfing session, Eddie scribbled outlines on sticky Post-it notes from work, pulled out his trusty four-track, and began to sing over the instrumentals.

He taped over a Merle Haggard *Best Of The 80's* cassette. He then used Wite-Out over all the info on the cassette cover, leaving only the title of a single track called *A Friend In California*, and letters spelling out "E-D-D-I-E".

Out came three songs in the form of a little rock opera, freely inspired by The Who's *Tommy* (a cornerstone of Eddie's musical education). A mini-opera about birth, incest, and death. In his rendition, *Dollar Short* was renamed *Alive* (Act One). In the autobiographical lyrics, Eddie sang about the lies surrounding his parentage, rounding out the developing storyline with some fiction about incest. *Alive*, Eddie explained to journalist Jessica Letkemann in 1999, was inspired by "a situation I felt I could draw from, this strange twist in my life having to do with a father that I didn't know was my father until later in my adolescent years. But what

I tried to do off that, was make it a little more interesting and turn it into more of a serial killer type scenario".

Agytian Crave turned into *Once* (Act Two). Here, the main character from *Alive* has turned into «a serial killer [who'd] been abused by his folks», thus provoking the «nasty things [he did] to other people». [32]

Troubled Times morphed into *Footsteps* (Act Three, final), where the protagonist finds himself in jail for his multiple crimes.

Eddie named the three-song package "Momma-Son", a variation on the term "mamasan", from a line in The Clash's *Straight to Hell.*

Ironically, just days after Eddie had sent the tape over to Seattle, he came across an issue of *Rolling Stone* that included Jeff and Stone's ad for a singer. They hadn't heard Eddie yet.

When the *Momma-Son* tape reached Jeff Ament's Queen Anne apartment around Tuesday, September 18th, he was blown away. He even listened to it multiple times, just to be sure it would have the same effect.

It did.

Jeff biked up to Stone's place in a hurry and made him listen to the tape too. They both agreed: Ed was their guy.

They arranged to fly him up to Seattle, mainly thanks to Michael Goldstone, who bankrolled the trip.

Formally, both Jeff and Stone were still bound to PolyGram. But Goldstone had recently shifted from PolyGram to Epic, and he was set on signing them to his new label. He played a pivotal role in freeing them from their previous contract.

On October 8th 1990, after laying down his vocals for *Alive* at The Potatohead's makeshift studios, Eddie Vedder

32 The reconstruction of events in the making of the *Momma-Son* tape is taken from *Music For Rhinos: The Making of Pearl Jam*, by Jessica Letkemann. TwoFeetThick.com Productions. bit.ly/3GscCIT.

quietly sat in a corner, watching Jeff and Stone rehearse with some other guys.

The band was called Temple Of The Dog, and it was a Seattle supergroup whose lineup included Jeff and Stone, plus Chris Cornell as the lead singer, guitarist Mike McCready and drummer Matt Cameron.

Half Mother Love Bone, half Soundgarden.

Eddie was told that Temple Of The Dog was the result of the death of a friend. Some sort of a high-powered tribute band [33].

Eddie knew about Andy. He knew he somehow had to fill his shoes. He knew every single person in that room, including himself, was dealing with some kind of devastating loss. The loss of a father, or the loss of a friend, who happened to be your band's lead singer.

Temple of The Dog were rehearsing a song called *Hunger Strike.*

Chris Cornell, on lead vocals, was having a hard time switching quickly between the high and low notes. So Eddie, "humbly - but with some balls", [34] walked up to the mic and started singing the low parts for Chris. They went through a couple of choruses like that and suddenly history had been written. *Hunger Strike* would end up featuring Vedder's vocals in its final version.

Both those tracks and more ended up in a self-titled album that was recorded and mixed in just fifteen days at London Bridge Studios. [35]

With that being said, Temple Of The Dog was *not* Ed-

33 "Temple Of The Dog" is taken from a line of a Mother Love Bone song called *Man of Golden Words*

34 Eric Weisbard, et al. *Ten Past Ten*, Spin, *August* 2001

35 *Temple of the Dog*, produced by Rick Parashar (who also contributed playing organ and piano), hit shelves on April 16th, 1991. The album got great reviews, but didn't chart. Temple of the Dog played two tiny Seattle gigs in late 1990, but there was no tour. The band (without Eddie Vedder) reunited and toured in 2016.

die's band. His band would be called Mookie Blaylock [36] and it would take shape in the space of just a week. The band rehearsed for five days, eight to ten hours a day, on ten songs, and then on the sixth day, November 13th, 1990, they played their very first gig at Seattle's Off Ramp Cafe.

They even took some time off to see the Chicago Bulls play the Seattle Supersonics at the Kingdome. [37]

Eventually Eddie would fly over back to Seattle on a one-way ticket. At that point, he knew his future would unfold right there.

Of all the songs included in the *Momma-Son* tape, one in particular, *Dollar Short*, had failed to enter *Apple*'s final tracklist, but, for some reason, that simple but charming guitar riff had kept on flowing out of Stone's fingers. He simply couldn't get rid of it.

During *Apple*'s recording sessions in Sausalito, that song had been rehearsed numerous times, but none of the band members had been able to make anything of it.

One night, while everybody was chilling in the condo after studio time, Stone had started strumming it on his guitar. Jeff was doing the dishes, Andy, sitting on the sofa, was watching football with his Dallas Cowboys hat on. Despite the game, Andy's ear was attracted to that riff. All of a sudden, he had started improvising on it, exactly as he had done while performing it live in Portland.[38]

36 The name pays homage to Daron Oshay *"Mookie" Blaylock*, a former NBA basketball player, whose jersey number was 10.

37 The genesis of Pearl Jam, taking shape in those very early days, has been reported slightly differently each time by each band member. A very detailed recollection of every single version has been accurately put together in Jessica Letkemann's *Music For Rhinos, The Making of Pearl Jam.* TwoFeetThick.com Productions. bit.ly/3GscCIT.

38 Proof of this episode is in an official private recording the author had access to. Thanks to Denny Swofford.

Pearl Jam, Ten Photoshoot, 1991. Photo by Lance Mercer

On October 22nd, 1990, Mookie Blaylock performed that song and others at Seattle's Off Ramp on their very first gig, opening for Alice in Chains.

When they took to the stage, an audience of around three hundred people wondered who that shy guy called Eddie was, filling Andy's shoes. Everybody was eager to see what Jeff and Stone's new band sounded like.

After a brief soundcheck performing a track called *Even Flow*, they kicked in with their set.

Right after performing the first riff of *Alive*, third song on the setlist, Mike McCready had a sort of epiphany. He knew right then and there, that it was the beginning of an amazing journey.

That *Dollar Short* song, the one nobody in Mother Love Bone could come to terms with, was not made for *Apple*.

It was made to be part of an album called Ten, and it would turn into a timeless banger, making your heart bleed

It would be titled *Alive*.

Malfunkshun- Kevin Wood and Jeff Stark @ the Flights Pub, Everett WA, February 2016

AKNOWLEDGEMENTS

The words you have read in this book are not only my own. I have absorbed and reported – sometimes quoting directly - what other people have told me. Without their contribution, I wouldn't have written a single page. In particular, I owe much to the following people:

Toni Wood, Andy's mother, for accepting to talk to me about her son, twenty-six years after his death. For having gifted me with an entire day spent roaming Bainbridge Island together. For painting a vivid family portrait with wonderful humor, that I hope I did justice to.

Kevin Wood, Andy's older brother and founder/guitarist of Malfunkshun. After Andy's passing, he went on with his music endeavours. In 1991 he formed The Fire Ants with his brother Brian and drummer Chad Channing. Later on, he co-founded Devilhead and, in 2002, he re-formed Malfunkshun, who are still a band. Occasionally, he would join Brad. Kevin's contribution to this book was essential to piece together the eventful life of the Wood family.

Brian Wood, Andy's brother, even though we never met I feel I should thank him because on various occasions his words inspired and moved me.

Bruce Fairweather, former guitarist of Mother Love Bone (previously Deranged Diction, Green River, then Love Battery), for opening the doors of his home in Seattle for a long group interview that retraced the story of Mother Love Bone. More than an interview, it was an informal stream-of-consciousness chat accompanied by a generous quantity of beer and crudités.

Greg Gilmore, former drummer of Mother Love Bone (previously of Ten Minute Warning), for subjecting himself to countless hours of interview by skype, for the quality time we spent together in Seattle, and for taking me to

Central Tavern and London Bridge Studios, two of the few places that have remained intact.

Stone Gossard, former guitarist of Mother Love Bone (previously March Of Crimes, Ducky Boys, Green River, then guitarist and founder of Pearl Jam), for talking to me at length about Andy, of the time between Mother Love Bone and the birth of Pearl Jam, and for allowing me to tell the origin story of *Dollar Short*.

Denny Swofford, archivist of Mother Love Bone, also known as "the man of many hats". His contribution was essential. I thank him for sharing precious recordings of Mother Love Bone from his personal archive, for the long conversations about Andy, and for enriching this book with never-before-seen photos.

Jack Endino, master producer of the Seattle scene, for the intense email exchange that allowed me to put together a timeline of Malfunkshun's recording sessions, for telling me about Kurt Cobain before his band was called Nirvana, and for the detailed account of the genesis of *Storm* by Soundgarden.

Regan Hägar, former drummer of Malfunkshun (later in Satchel and Brad), close friend of Andy's, for understanding the spirit of this book, and accepting to be interviewed, in spite of how painful the memories still are.

Mark Arm and **Steve Turner,** respectively voice and guitar of Mudhoney (previously in Green River), for welcoming me among their camp as if I were one of their own, at Bloom in Mezzago, Italy in May of 2015, and for sitting down for a long interview that retraced at least ten years of music in Seattle.

Jonathan Evison, writer (previously singer of March Of Crimes), for his constant counsel, in spite of his busy schedule presenting internationally renowned books (his own).

Michael Edward Browning, former reporter of *Rip Magazine*, for unearthing that very last interview with Andy, and for providing me with precious audio of Mother Love Bone.

Other people I'd like to thank for their precious contribution (in alphabetic order):

Dave Abbruzzese (Pearl Jam's former drummer, 1991 to 1994)

Joe Abrams (musician, close friend of Andy's) **Danny Baird** (former road manager for Mudhoney)

Fabrizio Coppola (italian singer songwriter, author, translator)

Charles R. Cross (music journalist, former editor of *The Rocket*, Nirvana's biographer)

Stuart Dahlquist (musician)

Ken Deans (former AIC manager, Mark Alan Production co-founder)

Pino Foderaro (co-founder of italian grunge community Aternative Grunge Crew)

Paul Hernandez (photographer)

Terry Lightening (Mother Love Bone die-hard fan who gave precious testimony of the scene as it was)

Mike Jones (radio DJ, formerly of KISW 99.9)

Charles Peterson (photographer)

Greg Prato (music journalist, writer)

Robert Scott Crane (actor, friend of Andy's)

Stephen Tow (journalist, writer)

Nicole Vandenberg (owner of Vandenberg Communications, Pearl Jam's management)

Kim Warnick (co-founder, voice and bassist of The Fastbacks)

Very special thanks to **Mark Wilkerson**, author (*Who Are You: The Life Of Pete Townshend/ Pearl Jam Twenty*), for encouraging me to make an English edition of this book available, and for his precious time and reviewing.

Special thanks go to **Valeria "Madreperla" Avesani**. For believing in this book, for being an amazing guide in Seattle and introducing me to some special people.

ESSENTIAL BIBLIOGRAPHY

Pearl Jam, Mark Wilkerson, Jonathan Cohen, *Pearl Jam Twenty*, Simon & Schuster, 2011.

Scot Barbour, *Malfunkshun. The Andrew Wood Story*, Universal – The Maze, *2005*

Michael Edward Browning – Karen Mason Blair, *1990: Seattle's Music Scene Distorts As 80's Glam Goes 90's Grunge*, Linkebook Publishing, 2012

Keith Cameron, *Mudhoney. The Sound And The Fury From Seattle*, Voyageur Press, 2014

Guido Chiesa – Steve Blush, *The Sound Of Seattle*, Stampa Alternativa – Nuovi Equilibri, 1993

Charles R. Cross, *Heavier Than Heaven. A Biography Of Kurt Cobain*, Hyperion, 2001

David De Sola, *Alice In Chains. The Untold Story*, Macmillan, 2015

Simone Dotto, *Pearl Jam – Still Alive. Testi Commentati*, Arcana Editore, 2014

Milena Ferrante, *Pearl Jam. Atto di rivolta*, Giunti Editore, 2003

Justin Henderson, *Grunge Seattle*, Roaring Forties Press, 2016

Jessica Letkemann, *1990 Music For Rhinos. The Making Of Pearl Jam*, Twofeetthick.com

Mike McCready, *Pearl Jam's Mike McCready Talks Kiss Obsession and Influence*, Rolling Stone, 3 aprile 2014

Duff McKagan, *It's So Easy And Other Lies*, Touchstone, 2011

Kim Neely, *Five Against One. The Pearl Jam Story*, Penguin Books, 1998

Chris Nickson, *Soundgarden. New Metal Crown*, St.Martin's Griffin, 1995

Greg Prato, *Grunge Is Dead. A Oral History Of Seattle Rock Music*, ECWPr, 2009

John Reynolds – Jessica Letkemann, *Inside The Stone Gossard Summer 1990 Demos*, TwoFeetthick, Pearl Jam For Impassioned Fan, ottobre 2010, www.twofeetthick.com/2010/10/13/stone-gossard-summer-1990-demos

Tom Scanlon, *Subpop's Got Some Kind Of Record*, The Seattle Times, 2008, seattletimes.com/entertainment/subpops-got-some-kind-of-record

Claudio Todesco, *Grunge. Il rock dalle strade di Seattle*, Tsunami Editore, 2011

Stephen Tow, *The Strangest Tribe. How A Group Of Seattle Rock Bands Invented Grunge*, Sasquatch Books, 2011

Katherine Turman, *Life Rules*, Rip Magazine, 1991

Richard T. White, *The Art of the Deal. How Mother Love Bone got one of the biggest record deals of the year*, The Rocket, gennaio 198

Mark Yarm, *Everybody Loves Our Town. A History Of Grunge*, Faber & Faber, 2011

"Sometimes, whether you like it or not, people elevate you (and) it's real easy to fall . . . "

- Eddie Vedder, Fairfax, VA, 04/08/1994

Lightning Source UK Ltd.
Milton Keynes UK
UKHW020620220822
407635UK00006B/542